SWU-700-010

# UNIFORMS OF RUSSIAN ARMY IN THE XVIII CENT. VOL.3

## UNDER THE REIGN OF CATHERINE II
### EMPRESSE OF RUSSIA BETWEEN 1762 AND 1796

From the Viskovatov's greatest work:
"Historical description of the clothing and
arms of the Russian Army"

## SOLDIERSHOP PUBLISHING

## AUTHOR

Aleksandr Vasilevich Viskovatov born 22 April (4 May New Style) 1804, died 27 February (11 March) 1858 in St. Petersburg, Russian military historian. He graduated from the 1st Cadet Corps and served in the artillery, the hydrographic depot of the Naval Ministry, and then in the Department of Military Educational Institutions. He mainly studied historical artifacts and the histories of military units. Viskovatov's greatest work was the Historical Description of the Clothing and Arms of the Russian Army.

Title: **UNIFORMS OF RUSSIAN ARMY IN THE XVIII Cent. VOL. 3 -**
**The Russian Army under the reign of Catherine the Great 1762-1796**
By A.V.Viskovatov. Serie edit by Luca S. Cristini. First edition by Soldiershop. September 2016
Cover & Art Design: Luca S. Cristini. Plates re-colorations by Anna Cristini.
ISBN code: 978-88-93272322
Published by Soldiershop publishing, via Padre Davide, 7 - 24050 Zanica (BG) ITALY. www.soldiershop.com

# UNIFORMS
# OF THE RUSSIAN ARMY IN
# THE XVIII Cent.
# VOL. 3

## UNDER THE REIGN OF CATHERINE II  EMPRESSE OF
## RUSSIA BETWEEN 1762 AND 1796

*Portrait of Catherine 2nd the Legislatress in the Temple of the Goddess of Justice. Work by Dmitry Levitsky*

# HISTORICAL DESCRIPTION OF THE CLOTHING AND ARMS
# OF THE RUSSIAN ARMY - A.V. VISKOVATOV

Soldiershop is glad to presents the complete collection of the great job made by A.V. Viskovatov dedicated to the uniforms and weapons belonging from the first Zar and Russian emperors to the Russian army during the Napoleonic period, until 1860 about. The time we considered in this volume corresponds to the reigns of Catherine the Great (Catherine II) who reigned since 1762 until his murder on the 6 November 1796.

Our reprint in based on the original 19th century volumes, to be precise the volumes from 4 to 6 are dedicated to the reign of Catherine II; this part is distributed on 3 or 4 volumes.

Our new edition, the first ever published in English, both on paper and digital format, boasts a large number of color plates, many of them unpublished and re-coloured by our team of expert artists and scholars of uniformology. Each volume is based on 100 color plates or more, always accompanied by the original translated text which describes the subjets of the plates.

A unique work in its genre, a must have in any respecting collection!

Aleksandr Vasilevich Viskovatov born 22 April (4 May New Style) 1804, died 27 February (11 March) 1858 in St. Petersburg, Russian military historian. He graduated from the 1st Cadet Corps and served in the artillery, the hydrographic depot of the Naval Ministry, and then in the Department of Military Educational Institutions.

He mainly studied historical artifacts and the histories of military units. Viskovatov's greatest work was the Historical Description of the Clothing and Arms of the Russian Army (Vols. 1-30, St. Petersburg, 1841-62; 2nd ed. Vols. 1-34, St. Petersburg - Novosibirsk - Leningrad, 1899-1948). This work is based on a great quantity of archival documents and contains four thousand colored illustrations.

Viskovatov was the author of Chronicles of the Russian Army (Books 1-20, St. Petersburg, 1834-42) and Chronicles of the Russian Imperial Army (Parts 1-7, St. Petersburg, 1852). He collected valuable material on the history of the Russian navy which went into A Short Overview of Russian Naval Campaigns and General Voyages to the End of the XVII Century (St. Petersburg, 1864; 2nd edition Moscow, 1946). Together with A.I. Mikhailovskii-Danilevskii he helped prepare and create the Military Gallery in the Winter Palace.

He wrote the historical military inscriptions for the walls of the Hall of St. George in the Great Palace of the Kremlin. (From the article in the Soviet Military Encyclopedia.)

# CONTENTS

*

# MEMOIRS OF THE EMPRESS CATHERINE II
## WRITTEN BY HERSELF - PART III.

### THIRD PART: FROM 1755, TO 1758

### 1755

Thus commenced the year 1755. From Christmas-day to Lent there was nothing but fêtes in the city and the court. It was still, in every case, in honour of the birth of my son that they were given. Every one in turn vied with his neighbour—all eager to give the most splendid dinners, balls, masquerades, illuminations, and fireworks. Under the plea of illness, I did not assist at any of them.

Towards the end of Lent, Serge Soltikoff returned from Sweden. During his absence, the High Chancellor, Count Bestoujeff, sent me all the news he received of him, as well as the despatches of Count Panine, at that time Envoy of Russia to the Swedish Court. They reached me through Madame Vladislava, who received them from her step-son, chief clerk to the High Chancellor, and I sent them back by the same way. I further learned by the same channel, that it was decided that on his return Soltikoff should be sent to Hamburg as resident minister of Russia, in place of Prince Alexander Galitzine, who was appointed to the army. This new arrangement did not diminish my sadness.

On his arrival, Serge Soltikoff requested me, through Leon Narichkine, to let him know if there was any possibility of his coming to see me. I spoke to Madame Vladislava, who consented to our interview. He was to come to her rooms, and thence to mine. I waited for him until three o'clock in the morning, and was in deadly anxiety as to what could have prevented his coming. I learned next day that he had been enticed by Count Roman Voronzoff into a lodge of Free Masons, and he pretended that he could not get away without giving rise to suspicions. But I questioned and cross-questioned Leon Narichkine to such a degree, that I saw as clear as the day that he had failed in his engagement from carelessness and want of interest, regardless of all I had so long suffered solely from my attachment to him.

Leon Narichkine himself, although his friend, did not offer much, if any excuse for him. To tell the truth, I was greatly annoyed, and wrote him a letter, in which I complained bitterly of his indifference. He answered it, and came to see me. He had little difficulty in appeasing me, for I was only too well disposed to accept his apologies.

He recommended me to go into public: I followed his advice, and made my appearance on the 10th of February, the birthday of the Grand Duke, as well as Shrove Tuesday. I had prepared for the occasion a superb dress of blue velvet, embroidered with gold. As during my solitude, I had thought a great deal, I now determined that, as far as depended on myself, I would make those who had occasioned me so many and such various annoyances, feel that I was not to be offended with impunity, and that it was not by ill-treatment they could hope to gain either my affection or approbation. In consequence, I neglected no opportunity of proving to the Schouvaloffs my feelings towards them.

I treated them with profound contempt, pointed out to others their stupidity and ill-nature, turned them into ridicule wherever I could, and had always some sarcasm ready to fling at them, which afterwards flew through the city, and gratified malignity at their expense: in a word, I took my revenge upon them in every way I could think of, and, in their presence, never failed to distinguish, by my attentions, those whom they disliked. As there were a great many people who hated them, I was never at a loss for subjects. The Counts Rasoumowsky, whom I had always liked, were caressed more than ever. I redoubled my politeness and attention to every one except the Schouvaloffs.

In a word, I drew myself up, and, with head erect, stood forth rather like the chief of a great party than a person humbled and oppressed. The Schouvaloffs knew not what to make of me. They took counsel, and had recourse to the tricks and intrigues of courtiers. At this time there appeared in Russia, one Brockdorf, a gentleman from Holstein, who, on a former visit, had been sent back over the frontiers, by the party then in power, Brummer and Berkholz, because he was known to be an intriguer, and a person of very bad character. This man came on the scene quite opportunely for the Schouvaloffs. As he had a key, as Chamberlain to the Grand Duke, in his character of Duke of Holstein, this gave him the entrée to his Imperial Highness, who, moreover, was favourably disposed towards every fool who came from that country.

Brockdorf gained an introduction to Count Peter Schouvaloff, in the following manner: In the inn where he lodged, he formed the acquaintance of a man who never left the inns of St. Petersburg unless it were to visit three young and rather pretty German girls, named Reifenstein, one of whom enjoyed a pension allowed her by Count Peter Schouvaloff. This man was called Braun; he was a kind of agent for all sorts of matters. He introduced Brockdorf at the house of these girls, where he formed the acquaintance of Count Peter Schouvaloff. The latter made great protestations of affection for the Grand Duke, and by degrees complained of me. All this M. Brockdorf reported to the Grand Duke, at the first opportunity, and they stirred him up until he determined, as he expressed it, to bring his wife to her senses. With this view, his Imperial Highness came into my room one day after dinner, and told me that I was becoming intolerably proud, but that he would bring me to my senses. I asked him in what my pride consisted.

He answered that I held myself very erect. I asked whether, in order to please him, I must stoop like the slaves of the Grand Seignior. He got angry, and said, he knew how to bring me to reason. I inquired how this was to be done.

Thereupon he placed his back against the wall, and half unsheathing his sword, showed it to me. I asked what he meant by that, for if he meant to fight me, why then I must have one too. He replaced his half-drawn sword in the scabbard, and told me that I had become dreadfully spiteful. "In what respect?" I said. He replied, with a stammer, "Why, to the Schouvaloffs." To this I answered that it was only tit for tat, and that he had better not meddle with matters which he knew nothing about, and could not understand. Upon this he exclaimed, "See what it is not to trust one's true friends; one suffers for it. If you had confided in me, it would have been well for you." "But in what should I have confided in you?" I said. Then he began talking in a manner so utterly extravagant, that finding it useless to reason with him, I let him go on without interruption, and seized a favourable moment to advise him to go to bed, for I saw clearly that wine had disturbed his reason and stupefied what little sense he naturally possessed.

He followed my advice, and retired. At this time he began to have always about him an odour of wine mingled with that of tobacco, which was really insupportable to all who came close to him. The same evening, while I was playing at cards, Count Alexander Schouvaloff came to me to signify, on behalf of the Empress, that she had forbidden the ladies to use in their dress certain articles of ornament specified in the announcement. To show him how far his Imperial Highness had corrected me, I laughed at him to his face, and told him he might have saved himself the trouble of notifying the order to me, since I never wore any ornaments which were displeasing to her Imperial Majesty; and that, besides, I did not make my merit consist in beauty nor in ornament, for that when the one had faded, the other was ridiculous, and that there was nothing permanent but character.

He listened to this to the end, winking his right eye, as was his custom, and then went off with his grimaces. I called the attention of those who were with me to this peculiarity, which I mimicked, making every one laugh.

A few days afterwards the Grand Duke told me he wished to ask the Empress for money for his affairs in Holstein, which were getting worse and worse every day, and that Brockdorf had advised him to do so. I saw very clearly that they were but holding out a bait to him, to make him hope for this money through the intervention of the Schouvaloffs. I asked if there was no means of managing without it. He said he would show me the representations which had been made to him from Holstein, on that head. He did so, and after perusing the papers which he laid before me, I said that it seemed to me he might manage without going begging to his aunt, who, besides, might refuse him, as she had given him, not six months ago, 100,000 roubles. However he kept to his own opinion, and I to mine.

For a long time he was buoyed up with hopes, but in the end he got nothing.

After Easter we went to Oranienbaum. Before we set off, the Empress allowed me to see my son for the third time since his birth. It was necessary to go through all the apartments of her Imperial Majesty to get to his chamber, where I found him in a stifling heat, as I have already mentioned. On reaching the country we witnessed a phenomenon.

His Imperial Highness—though his Holstein subjects were continually preaching to him of a deficit, while everybody was advising him to diminish his useless retinue, which, after all, he could only see by stealth and piecemeal—suddenly took the daring resolution of bringing over an entire detachment. This again was a contrivance of that wretch Brockdorf, who flattered the ruling passion of the Prince. To the Schouvaloffs he represented that, by conniving at this hobby, they would for ever ensure his favour, make him wholly theirs, and be certain of his approbation in whatever they undertook. From the Empress, who detested Holstein, and all that came from it, who had seen how similar military crotchets had ruined the Grand Duke's father, the Duke Charles Frederick, in the opinion of Peter I. and of the Russian public, it would seem that the matter was so far concealed as to be represented to her as a mere trifle, not worth speaking of; while, besides, the mere presence of Count Schouvaloff was sufficient to prevent the affair from assuming any consequence.

Having embarked at Kiel, the detachment landed at Cronstadt, and then marched to Oranienbaum. The Grand Duke, who in Tchoglokoff's time had never worn the Holstein uniform, except in his own room, and by stealth, as it were, now wore no other, except on court days, although he was lieutenant-colonel of the Preobrajensky regiment, and had besides a regiment of cuirassiers in Russia. From me, the Grand Duke, by Brockdorf's advice, kept the transport of these troops a great secret. I own that when I became aware of it, I shuddered at the injurious effect which such a proceeding could not fail to have on the minds of the Russian people, as well as in the opinion of the Empress, of whose sentiments I was not at all ignorant. M. Alexander Schouvaloff saw the detachment defile before the balcony at Oranienbaum, winking all the while: I was by his side. In his heart he disapproved of what he and his relations had agreed to tolerate. The guard of the Château of Oranienbaum belonged to the regiment of Inguermanie, which alternated with that of Astracan. I was informed that, when they saw the Holstein troops pass, they muttered, "Those cursed Germans are all sold to the King of Prussia; it is so many traitors they are bringing into Russia." Generally speaking, the public was shocked at the apparition; the more earnest shrugged their shoulders, the more moderate looked upon it as simply ridiculous; in reality, it was a childish freak, but a very imprudent one. As for me, I was silent, though, when the matter was mentioned to me, I spoke my mind in such a manner as to show that I in no way approved of a proceeding which, under every point of view, could not but be injurious to the Grand Duke's interests. In fact, how was it possible to arrive at any other conclusion? His mere pleasure could not compensate for the injury which such a proceeding must do him in public opinion. But the Duke, enchanted with his troop, took up his quarters in the camp which he had prepared for it, where he was constantly employed in exercising it. At last it required to be fed; but this had not been thought of. The matter, however, was pressing, and there were some debates with the Marshal of the Court, who was not prepared for such a demand. At last he yielded, and the servants of the Court, with the soldiers of the Inguermanie regiment, on guard at the château, were employed in conveying provisions for the newly arrived, from the kitchen of the château to the camp. The camp was at some distance from the house; neither the servants nor the soldiers received anything for their trouble; one may easily understand the effect of so sapient an arrangement. The soldiers said, "They make us lackeys to those cursed Germans." The servants said, "We have to wait upon a set of clowns."

When I saw and heard what was going on, I resolved to keep myself at as great a distance as possible from this mischievous child's-play. The gentlemen of our court, who were married, had their wives with them; this made up a tolerably numerous company; no one, not even the gentlemen, would have anything to do with this Holstein Camp, which the Grand Duke never left. Thus, surrounded by these courtiers, I was out as much as possible, but always on the side opposite to the camp, which we never, by any chance, came near.

It was at this time that I took a fancy to form a garden at Oranienbaum, and as I knew that the Grand Duke would not give me an inch of ground for that purpose, I begged Prince Galitzine to sell or cede to me about one hundred toises of some waste land which belonged to his family in the immediate vicinity of Oranienbaum, and had been long since abandoned. This land was owned by eight or ten members of the family, but as it produced nothing, they willingly gave it up to me. I began then to plan and plant, and as this was my first whim in the constructive line, my plans assumed very grand proportions. My old surgeon Gyon, seeing these things, said to me, "What is the good of all this? Now, mark my words; I prophesy that you will one day abandon all this." His prediction was verified. But I required some amusement at the time, and this exercise of imagination was one. At first I employed, in planting my garden, the gardener of Oranienbaum, whose name was Lamberti. He had been in the service of the Empress, when she was princess, on her estate at Zarskoe-Selo, whence he had been removed to Oranienbaum. He was fond of predictions, and, among others, his prediction relative to the Empress had been fulfilled. He had prophesied that she would ascend the throne. He told me, and repeated it as often as I was willing to listen to him, that I should become the Sovereign Empress of Russia; that I should see sons, grandsons, and great-grandsons; and that I should die at the advanced age of more than fourscore years. He did more: he fixed the year of my accession to the throne six years before the event. He was a very singular man, and one who spoke with an assurance which nothing could disturb. He pretended that the Empress was ill-disposed towards him, because he had foretold to her what had come to pass, and that she had removed him from Zarskoe-Selo to Oranienbaum in consequence of being afraid of him.

It was at Whitsuntide, I think, that we were recalled from Oranienbaum to the city; and it was about the same time that the English Ambassador, the Chevalier Williams, came to Russia. He had in his suite Count Poniatowsky, a Pole, the son of the one who had followed the fortunes of Charles XII. of Sweden. After a short stay at the capital, we returned to Oranienbaum, where the Empress ordered us to keep the Festival of St. Peter. She did not come herself, because she did not wish to celebrate the first fête of my son Paul, which fell on the same day. She remained at Peterhoff, and there placed herself at a window, where she remained, it would seem, the whole day; for all who came to Oranienbaum said they had seen her at that window. A very large company assembled. The dance took place in the hall at the entrance of my garden, and we afterwards supped there. The foreign ambassadors and ministers were present.

I remember that the English Ambassador, the Chevalier Williams, sat near me at supper, and that we kept up a conversation as agreeable as it was gay. As he was lively and well-informed, it was not difficult to carry on a conversation with him. I afterwards learned that he had been as much pleased as myself at this soirée and had spoken of me in high terms. This, indeed, was what always happened when I chanced to be with those who suited me in mind and character, and, as at that time, I did not excite so much envy, I was generally well spoken of.

I was looked upon as a woman of mind; and many of those more intimately acquainted with me, honoured me with their confidence, depended on me, asked my advice, and found themselves the better for following it.

The Grand Duke had long since named me Madame la Ressource, and however angry or sulky he might be, if he found himself at a loss on any point, he would come running to me, in his usual style, to get my advice, and then be off again as fast as he could. I likewise remember, at this same feast of St. Peter, at Oranienbaum, seeing Count Poniatowsky dancing, and I spoke to the Chevalier Williams about his father, and the mischief he had done to Peter I.

The English Ambassador spoke very favourably of the son, and confirmed to me what I was already aware of, namely, that his father and the Czartoriskys, his mother's family, then formed the Russian party in Poland; that the son had been placed under his care, and sent here in order to be brought up in the feelings of his family towards Russia; and that they trusted he would succeed in this country. He might then be about twenty-two or twenty-three years old. I replied that, in general, I looked upon Russia as the stumbling-block of merit for strangers, and considered that those who succeeded in Russia might safely calculate upon success in every other part of Europe. This rule I have always considered as infallible, for nowhere are people more quick in detecting the weak points, absurdities, and defects of a stranger than in Russia. A stranger may be sure that nothing will be overlooked, for, naturally, no Russian really likes a foreigner.

About this time, I learned that the conduct of Sergius Soltikoff had been anything but prudent, whether in Sweden or at Dresden. Besides, he had made love to all the women he met. At first I would not believe these reports; but at last they came from so many quarters, that even his friends could not exculpate him. This year I became more than ever attached to Anne Narichkine. Her brother-in-law, Leon, contributed much to this. He always made a third with us, and there was no end to his nonsense. He used sometimes to say to us, "I have a bijou, which I mean to give to whichever of you two shall behave the best, and you will be very much obliged to me for it." We let him talk on, without troubling ourselves to inquire what this bijou was.

In the autumn, the Holstein troops were sent off by sea, and we went to occupy the Summer Palace. At this time Leon Narichkine fell ill of a burning fever, during which he sent me letters, which I could easily see were not his own.

I replied to him. In these letters he asked me for sweetmeats and such like trifles, and then returned thanks. The letters were very well written, and very lively; he said he employed in them the hand of his secretary. This secretary, I at last learned was Count Poniatowsky, who never left him, and had become intimate with his family. From the Summer Palace we removed, about the beginning of winter, to the new Winter Palace which the Empress had just built.

It was of wood, and occupied the spot where the mansion of the Tchitcherines now stands. It took up the whole quarter as far as the residence of the Countess Matiouchkine, which then belonged to Naoumoff. My windows faced this house, which was occupied by the maids of honour. On entering the apartments destined for us, I was very much struck with their size and loftiness. Four large ante-chambers and two chambers, with a cabinet, were prepared for me, and the same number for the Grand Duke. The rooms, too, were so disposed, that I was not incommoded by the proximity of the Grand Duke's apartments. This was a great point gained. Count Alexander Schouvaloff noticed my satisfaction, and immediately informed the Empress that I was greatly delighted with the number and size of my apartments.

This he told me afterwards with a kind of satisfaction, indicated by a smile and the winking of his eye.

At this period, and for a long time afterwards, the principal plaything of the Grand Duke, while in town, consisted of an immense number of little dolls, representing soldiers, formed of wood, lead, pith, and wax. These he arranged on very narrow tables, which took up an entire room, leaving scarcely space enough to pass between them.

Along these tables he had nailed narrow bands of brass, to which strings were attached, and when he pulled these strings the brass bands made a noise which, according to him, resembled the roll of musketry. He observed the court festivals with great regularity, making these troops produce their rolling fire; besides which he daily relieved guard, that is to say,

*British caricature of an attempted mediation between Catherine (on the right, supported by Austria and France) and Turkey*

from every table was picked out the dolls that were assumed to be on guard. He assisted at this parade in full uniform, boots, spurs, gorget, and scarf. Such of his domestics as were admitted to this precious exercise were obliged to appear in similar style.

Towards the winter of this year, I thought myself again pregnant. I was bled. I had a cold, or, rather, I fancied I had one, in both sides of my face; but after some days of suffering, four double teeth made their appearance at the four extremities of my jaws. As our apartments were very spacious, the Grand Duke had every week a ball and a concert.

The only persons who appeared at them were the maids of honour and the gentlemen of our court, together with their wives. These balls were thought interesting by those who assisted at them, who were never many.

The Narichkines were more companionable than the rest. Among them I reckon Madame Siniavine and Madame Ismaïloff, Leon's sisters, together with the wife of his elder brother, of whom I have already spoken.

Leon, more absurd than ever, and regarded by every one as a person of no sort of consequence, as was indeed the case, had got into the habit of running continually backwards and forwards between the Grand Duke's apartments and mine, never stopping long anywhere. In order to gain admittance into my room, he used to mew like a cat at my door, and when I answered him, he would come in. On the 17th of December, between six and seven o'clock in the evening, he announced himself in this fashion, at my door; I desired him to come in. He began by presenting me with his sister-in-law's compliments, saying that she was not well; and adding, "but you ought to go and see her."

I replied, "I would do so with pleasure; but you know I cannot go out without permission, and they will never give me permission to go to her house." "Oh! I will take you there," he said. "Are you mad," I replied; "how can I go with you? You would be sent to the Fortress, and God knows what trouble I should get into." "Oh! but no one will know of it; we will take proper precautions." "But how?" "Why, in this way: I will come and fetch you in an hour or two's time.

The Grand Duke will take supper" (for a long time past, under the pretext of not wishing for supper, I had been in the habit of staying in my own room); "he will remain at table for a considerable part of the night, leave it very tipsy, and go to bed" (since my confinement he generally slept in his own room); "for greater security you can dress in man's clothes, and we will go together to Anna Nikitichna Narichkine's." I began to feel tempted by the adventure, for I was constantly in my room with my books, and without any company. Finally, by dint of debating this mad project, for such it really was, and such it appeared to me at first, I saw in it the possibility of obtaining a moment's relaxation and amusement.

He departed, and I called a Kalmuck hair-dresser in my service, and desired him to bring me one of my male dresses, and all belonging to it, as I wanted to make it a present to some one. This young man was one of those persons who keep their mouths closed; and it was more difficult to make him speak than it was to make others hold their tongues.

He executed his commission promptly, and brought me everything I wanted. I feigned a headache, and went to bed early. As soon as Madame Vladislava had undressed me and retired, I got up and dressed myself from head to foot as a man, arranging my hair in the best way I could. I was long in the habit of doing this, and was by no means awkward at it.

At the time appointed, Narichkine made his appearance. He came through the apartments of the Grand Duke, and mewed at my door. I opened it, and we passed through a small ante-chamber into the hall, and entered his carriage without having been seen by any one, laughing like a pair of fools at our escapade. Leon lived in the same house with his brother and sister-in-law.

On reaching it, we found there Anna Nikitichna, who suspected nothing, and also Count Poniatowsky.

Leon announced one of his friends, whom he begged might be well received, and the evening passed in the wildest gayety. After a visit of an hour and-a-half's duration, I took leave and returned home without accident, and without having been met by any one. The next day, which was the birthday of the Empress, both at court in the morning, and at the ball in the evening, we could not look one another in the face without being ready to burst out laughing at our last night's folly. Some days later, Leon prepared a return visit, which was to take place in my apartments; and, as before, he brought his company into my room so skilfully, that no suspicion was excited. Thus began the year 1756.

We took a strange delight in these furtive interviews. Not a week passed without one or two, and occasionally even three of them taking place, sometimes at the residence of one party, sometimes at that of another; and if any of us happened to be ill, the visit was always to the invalid.

Sometimes at the theatre, without speaking, and simply by means of certain signs previously agreed on, even although we might be in different boxes, and some of us, perhaps, in the pit; yet, by a sign, each one knew where to go, and no mistake ever occurred between us, except that on two occasions I had to return home on foot, which, after all, was only a walk.

# 1756

At this period, preparations were making for a war with Prussia. The Empress, by her treaty with the house of Austria, was bound to furnish a contingent of thirty thousand men. Such was the view taken by the High Chancellor Count Bestoujeff; but Austria wanted Russia to aid her with all her forces. Count Esterhazy, the Austrian Ambassador, was intriguing for this object with all his skill, wherever he saw an opening, and often in several different channels at once.

The party opposed to Bestoujeff consisted of the Vice-Chancellor Count Voronzoff and the Schouvaloffs. England was at that time in alliance with Prussia, and France with Austria. The Empress began to have frequent indispositions.

At first it was not known what was the matter with her. The Schouvaloffs were often seen to be very much disturbed, and full of intrigues, and from time to time they paid great attentions to the Grand Duke. The courtiers whispered that these indispositions of her Imperial Majesty were much more serious than was reported.

Some called them hysterical affections, others fainting fits, or convulsions, or nervous complaints.

This state of things lasted the whole winter of 1755-1756. Finally, in the spring we learned that Marshal Apraxine was about to depart in command of the army that was to enter Prussia. His lady came to take leave of us, accompanied by her youngest daughter. I mentioned to her my apprehensions relative to the health of the Empress, stating that I much regretted the absence of her husband at a time in which I thought that little reliance was to be placed upon the Schouvaloffs, whom I looked upon as my personal enemies, and who were very ill-disposed towards me, because I preferred their enemies to them, and especially the Counts Razoumowsky.

She repeated all this to her husband, who was much pleased with my feelings towards him; so also was Count Bestoujeff, who disliked the Schouvaloffs, and was connected with the Razoumowskys, his son having married their niece.

Marshal Apraxine might have been a useful mediator between all interested, on account of the liaison of his daughter with Count Peter Schouvaloff: Leon pretended that this liaison was carried on with the knowledge of her parents.

Besides this, I saw clearly that the Schouvaloffs made more use than ever of M. Brockdorf, for the purpose of estranging the Grand Duke from me as much as possible. Notwithstanding all this, he had still an involuntary confidence in me; this he always retained to a remarkable extent, without being at all conscious of it himself. He had just then quarrelled with the Countess Voronzoff, and was in love with Madame Teploff, a niece of the Razoumowskys. When he wished to see this lady, he consulted me as to the best mode of adorning his room so as to please her, and made me observe that he had filled it with muskets, grenadier caps, shoulder belts, etc., so that it looked like a portion of an arsenal.

I let him do as he pleased, and went away. Besides this lady, he also kept a little German singing girl, called Leonora, who used to come to him of an evening, and sup with him. It was the Princess of Courland who had led to his quarrel with the Countess Voronzoff. Indeed, I do not very well know how it was that this Princess of Courland managed at that time to play a peculiar part at court. In the first place, she was then nearly thirty years of age, little, ugly, and humpbacked, as I have already said. She had contrived to secure the protection of the confessor of the Empress, and of several old ladies of her Majesty's bed-chamber, so that every thing she did was excused, and she remained among the Empress' maids of honour. All these were under the rod of a Madame Schmidt, the wife of one of the court trumpeters.

This Madame Schmidt was a native of Finland, prodigiously large and massive, one who knew how to ensure obedience, but who still retained the coarse and vulgar manners of her former condition. She was of some consequence, however, at court, being under the immediate protection of the Empress' old German and Swedish lady's-maids, and consequently also under that of the Marshal of the Court, Sievers, who was himself a Fin, and married to a daughter of Madame Krause, whose sister, as I have already mentioned, was one of those lady's-maids, and one in special favour with the Empress. Madame Schmidt ruled within the dwelling of the maids of honour with more vigour than intelligence, but never appeared at court. In public, the Princess of Courland was at their head, and Madame Schmidt had tacitly confided to her their conduct at court. In their own house, they all lodged in a row of chambers, which terminated at one end in Madame Schmidt's room, and at the other in the one occupied by the Princess of Courland.

There were two, three, or four in a room, each having a screen round her bed, and the only exits from these rooms were through each other. At first sight, it would seem that this arrangement made the residence of the maids of honour impenetrable, for it could only be reached by passing through Madame Schmidt's, or the Princess of Courland's room. But Madame Schmidt often suffered from the indigestion occasioned by all the pâtes gras and other dainties sent to her by the relatives of these young ladies, and then the only approach was by the Princess of Courland's chamber.

Here scandal reported that it was necessary for those who wished to pass to any of the rooms beyond, to pay toll in some form or other. At all events, it was certain that for many years the Princess of Courland made up matches and broke them off again—promised and refused the Empress' maids of honour just as she thought proper; and I have heard from the lips of many persons, and among others from Leon Narichkine and Count Boutourline, the history of this toll, which, they pretended had not in their case been paid in money.

The Grand Duke's amours with Madame Teploff lasted until we went into the country. Here they were interrupted, because his Imperial Highness was insupportable during the summer. Not being able to see him, Madame Teploff pretended that he must write to her at least once or twice a-week, and to induce him to do so, she began by writing him a letter of four pages. On receiving it, he came into my room much out of temper, holding the letter in his hand, and said to me, in a tone of considerable irritation, "Only fancy! she writes me a letter of four whole pages, and expects that I should read it, and, what is more, answer it also. I who have to go to parade (he had again brought his troops from Holstein), then dine, then shoot, then attend the rehearsal of an opera, and the ballet which the cadets will dance at it! I will tell her plainly that I have not time, and if she is vexed, I will quarrel with her till winter."

I told him that would certainly be the shortest way. These traits are, I think, characteristic, and they will not therefore be out of place. Here is the explanation of the appearance of the cadets at Oranienbaum.

In the spring of 1756, the Schouvaloffs thought, that with a view of detaching the Grand Duke from his Holstein troops, it would be a good stroke of policy to persuade the Empress to give his Imperial Highness the command of the corps of Land Cadets, the only body of cadets then existing. Under him was placed A. P. Melgounoff, the intimate friend and confidant of Ivan Ivanovitch Schouvaloff. This person was married to one of the German lady's-maids, a favourite of the Empress. In this way the Schouvaloffs had one of their most intimate friends in the Grand Duke's chamber, and with the opportunity of speaking to him at every moment. Under pretext of the opera-ballets at Oranienbaum, they brought there some hundred cadets, together with M. Melgounoff and the officers of the corps who were most intimate with him. These were so many spies à la Schouvaloff. Among the masters who came to Oranienbaum with the cadets was their riding-master, Zimmerman, who was accounted the best horseman at that time in Russia.

As my supposed pregnancy of the last autumn had all passed off, I thought I would take some lessons in horsemanship from Zimmerman. I spoke on the subject to the Grand Duke, who made no difficulty. For a long time past all the old rules introduced by the Tchoglokoffs were forgotten, neglected by, or altogether unknown to Alexander Schouvaloff, who, besides, was held in slight or no consideration: we laughed at him, at his wife, his daughter, and his son-in-law, almost to their faces. They gave abundant room for it; for never were faces more ignoble or mean looking than theirs.

I had applied to Madame Schouvaloff the epithet of the "pillar of salt." She was thin, and short, and stiff. Her avarice showed itself even in her dress. Her petticoats were always too narrow, and had a breadth less than was required, and than those of other ladies had. Her daughter, the Countess Golofkine, was similarly dressed.

Their head-dresses and ruffles were mean, and had a look of stinginess about them, although these people were very wealthy, and in all respects in easy circumstances. But they naturally liked everything that was little and pinched—a true image of their minds.

As soon as I came to take lessons in systematic riding, I again became passionately fond of this exercise.

I rose every morning at six, dressed myself in male attire, and went off to my garden, where I had a place prepared in the open air, which served me for a riding-school. I made such rapid progress, that Zimmerman frequently came running up to me with tears in his eyes, and kissed my foot with a sort of uncontrollable enthusiasm.

At other times he would exclaim, "Never in my life have I had a pupil who did me such credit, or who made such rapid progress in so short a time." At these lessons, there was no one present but my old surgeon Gyon, a lady's-maid and some domestics. As I paid great attention to these lessons, and took them regularly every morning except Sundays, Zimmerman rewarded my diligence with the silver spurs, which he gave me, according to the rules of the school.

By the end of three weeks I had passed through all the gradations of the school, and towards autumn Zimmerman had a leaping-horse bought, after which he intended to give me the stirrups. But the day before that fixed for my mounting, we received orders to return to town; the matter was therefore put off till the following spring.

During this summer Count Poniatowsky made a tour in Poland, from which he returned with his credentials as minister of the King of Poland. Before his departure he came to Oranienbaum, to take leave of us. He was accompanied by Count Horn, whom the King of Sweden, under the pretext of notifying the death of his mother, my grandmother, had sent to Russia, in order to withdraw him from the persecutions of the French party, otherwise called "The Hats," against that of Russia, or "The Caps." This persecution became so fierce in Sweden at the diet of 1756, that almost all the chiefs of the Russian party had their heads cut off this year. Count Horn told me himself, that if he had not come to Russia, he would certainly have been of the number.

Count Poniatowsky and Count Horn remained two days at Oranienbaum. The first day the Grand Duke treated them very well, but on the second they were in his way, for his thoughts were running on the wedding of one of his huntsmen, at which he wished to be present for the purpose of drinking. Finding that his guests still stayed, he left them there, and I had to do the honours of the house.

After dinner, I took the company which had remained with us, and which was not very numerous, to view the interior of the house. On reaching my cabinet, a little Italian greyhound that I had there, ran to meet us, and began to bark loudly at Count Horn, but when he perceived Count Poniatowsky, he seemed wild with delight.

As the cabinet was very small, no one observed this but Leon Narichkine, his sister-in-law and myself. But it did not escape the notice of Count Horn, and while I was going through the apartments to return to the saloon, Count Horn took Poniatowsky by the coat and said to him, "My friend, there is nothing so terrible as a little Italian greyhound; the first thing I always do with the ladies I am in love with is to give them one of these little dogs, and by this means I can always discover whether there is any one more favoured than myself. The rule is infallible. You see it.

The dog growled as if he would have eaten me, because I am a stranger, while he was mad with joy when he saw you again, for most assuredly this is not the first time he has seen you there." Count Poniatowsky treated all this as an absurdity on his part, but he could not dissuade him. Count Horn merely replied, "Fear nothing; you have to deal with a discreet person." Next morning they departed. Count Horn used to say, that when he went so far as to fall in love, it was always with three women at a time. And we had an example of this under our eye at St. Petersburg, where he courted three young ladies at once. Count Poniatowsky left two days afterwards for Poland.

During his absence the Chevalier Williams sent me word, through Leon Narichkine, that the High Chancellor Bestoujeff was caballing against the nomination of Count Poniatowsky, and had, through him, endeavoured to dissuade Count Bruhl, at that time the minister and favourite of the King of Poland, from making it.

He added that he took care not to fulfil this commission, although he had not declined it, fearing it might be given to some one else, who would probably discharge it more exactly, and thus prejudice his friend, who wished, above all things, to return to Russia. The Chevalier suspected that Count Bestoujeff, who for a long time had the Saxo-Polish ministers at his disposal, wished to nominate to that post some person particularly in his confidence. However, Count Poniatowsky obtained the appointment, and returned, towards winter, as Envoy of Poland, while the Saxon embassy remained under the immediate direction of Count Bestoujeff.

Some time before we quitted Oranienbaum, the Prince and Princess Galitzine arrived there, accompanied by M. Betzky. They were going to travel abroad on account of ill-health, especially Betzky, who needed some distraction to relieve the deep melancholy into which he had been plunged by the death of the Princess of Hesse Homburg—born Princess Troubetzkoy, mother of the Princess Galitzine, who was the issue of the first marriage of the Princess of Hesse with the Hospodar of Wallachia, Prince Kantemir. As the Princess Galitzine and Betzky were old acquaintances, I endeavoured to give them the best reception I could at Oranienbaum, and after having shown them about a good deal, the Princess Galitzine and I got into a cabriolet, which I guided myself, and we took a drive in the neighbourhood of Oranienbaum. On our way, the Princess, who was a very singular and narrow-minded person, gave me to understand that she thought I entertained some ill-feeling against her. I assured her that such was not the case, and that I did not know of anything which could give occasion to any ill-feeling on my part, as I had never had any disagreement with her. Thereupon she told me that she had feared Count Poniatowsky might have injured her in my good opinion. I thought I should have dropped at these words. I replied that she must certainly be dreaming; that the person she spoke of was not in a position to prejudice her in my opinion; that he had been gone some time; that I only knew him by sight, and as a stranger; and that I could not understand what could have put such an idea into her head. Upon my return home, I sent for Leon Narichkine, and related to him this conversation, which appeared to me as stupid as it was impertinent and indiscreet. He told me that during last winter the Princess Galitzine had moved heaven and earth to attract Count Poniatowsky to her house, and that he out of politeness, and not to be wanting in respect, had paid her some attention; that she had made all sort of advances to him, to which it may easily be believed he did not much respond, as she was old, ugly, stupid, and foolish—indeed, almost crazy; and that seeing she could make no impression on him, her suspicions seemed to have been excited by the fact that he was always with him, Narichkine, and at his sister-in-law's house.

During the brief stay of the Countess Galitzine at Oranienbaum, I had a dreadful quarrel with the Grand Duke about my maids of honour. I had observed that these ladies, who were always either confidantes or mistresses of the Grand Duke, had on several occasions been neglectful of their duties, or even failed in the respect and deference which they owed me. I went one afternoon into their apartment, and reproached them with their conduct, reminding them of their duty, of what they owed me, telling them if they went on in the same way I should complain to the Empress.

Some of them were alarmed, others got angry, and some wept; but as soon as I was gone, they immediately hurried to the Grand Duke, and told him what I had said to them. His Imperial Highness got furious, and immediately running to my room, exclaimed that there was no living with me; that every day I became more proud and haughty; that I demanded of the maids of honour attentions and deferences which embittered their lives; that I made them cry all day long; that they were ladies of rank, whom I treated like servants; and if I complained of them to the Empress, he would complain of me—of my pride, my arrogance, my ill-nature, and God knows what besides. I listened to him, not without agitation, and replied that he might say of me whatever he pleased; that if the affair was carried before his aunt, she would be able to judge whether it would not be well to dismiss from my service women of bad conduct, who, by their tittle-tattle, caused dissension between her nephew and niece; for that if she wished to restore peace between us, and prevent her ears from being perpetually dinned with our quarrels, she could not adopt any other course; and that, consequently, this would certainly be the course she would adopt. At this he lowered his tone, fancying (for he was very suspicious) that I knew more of the intentions of the Empress with regard to these women than I allowed to appear, and that in reality they might all be dismissed for this business. He therefore said, "Tell me, then; do you know anything on this point? Has any one spoken to her of them?" I replied that if matters went so far as to come before the Empress, I had no doubt she would dispose of them in a very summary manner. At this he began walking with hasty strides up and down my room in a reverie; gradually cooled down; and then went away, only half-sulky. The same evening, I related this conversation, word for word, to one of these maids of honour, who appeared to me more sensible than the rest, and described the scene which their imprudent tattling had caused. This put them on their guard against carrying matters to an extremity, of which, probably, they would become the victims.

During the autumn we returned to town, and shortly afterwards the Chevalier Williams left for England on leave. He had failed in his object in Russia. The very next day after his audience of the Empress, he had proposed a treaty of alliance between England and Russia. Count Bestoujeff had orders and full authority to conclude this treaty. In fact, the treaty was signed by him, and the Ambassador could scarcely contain his joy at his success, but the following day Count Bestoujeff communicated to him, by note, the accession of Russia to the convention signed at Versailles between France and Austria. This was a thunderbolt for the English Ambassador, who had been played with and deceived in this affair by the High Chancellor, or appeared to have been so. But Count Bestoujeff himself could no longer do as he pleased; his opponents were beginning to get the upper hand of him, and they intrigued, or rather others were intriguing with them, to gain them over to the Franco-Austrian party, to which they were already much disposed.

The Schouvaloffs, and especially Ivan Ivanovitch, had a passion for France and all that belonged to it, and in this they were seconded by the Vice-Chancellor Voronzoff, for whom Louis XV. in return for this piece of service, furnished the mansion which he had just built at St. Petersburg, with old furniture which his mistress, Madame Pompadour, had become tired of, and had sold to her lover, the King, at a good price. But apart from all considerations of profit, the Vice-Chancellor had another motive: he wished to lessen the credit of his rival, Count Bestoujeff, and secure his place for Peter Schouvaloff. Besides, he meditated a monopoly of the Russian trade in tobacco, in order to sell the article in France.

# 1757

Towards the end of the year, Count Poniatowsky returned to Russia as minister of the King of Poland. In the early part of the year, the tenor of our life was the same as in the previous winter; the same balls, the same concerts, and the same coteries. Soon after our return to the city, where I could observe things more closely, I perceived that M. Brockdorf, with his intrigues, was making rapid progress in the good graces of the Grand Duke. He was seconded in this by a considerable number of Holstein officers whom he had encouraged his Highness to retain this winter at St. Petersburg.

The number amounted to at least twenty, who were continually within the Grand Duke's circle, without counting a couple of Holstein soldiers who did duty in his chamber as messengers, valets-de-chambre—factotums, in a word.

All these were, in reality, so many spies in the service of Messrs. Brockdorf and Co. I watched for a favourable moment during this winter to speak seriously to the Grand Duke, and tell him exactly what I thought of those about him, and of the intrigues which I saw going on. One presented itself, which I did not neglect. The Grand Duke himself came one day into my cabinet, to tell me that it had been represented to him as indispensably necessary that he should send secret orders to Holstein for the arrest of a person named Elendsheim, who, by his office and the personal consideration he enjoyed, was one of the leading men of the country. He was of bourgeois extraction, but had risen by his learning and capacity to his present post. I asked the Duke what complaints were made against him, and what he had done to require his arrest. He replied, "Why, you see, they tell me he is suspected of malversation." I inquired who were his accusers.

On this, he thought himself very reasonable in saying, "Oh, as for accusers, there are none, for every one in the country fears and respects him; and it is on this very account that I ought to have him arrested, for as soon as this is done, there will be, I am assured, accusers enough and to spare." I shuddered at this answer, and replied, "But at this rate there will not be an innocent man in the world; it will only be necessary for some envious person to set afloat any vague rumour he pleases, and then any one whatever may be arrested on the principle that accusations and crimes will come afterwards. It is, to use the words of the song, 'à la façon de Barbari, mon ami,' that they are advising you to act, without regard to your reputation or your sense of justice. Who is it that gives you such bad advice? if I may be allowed to ask."

My gentleman looked a little foolish at this question, and said, "You are always wanting to know more than other people." I replied, that it was not for the sake of knowing that I spoke, but because I hated injustice, and could not believe that he wished to commit such a wrong out of mere wantonness. Upon this he began to pace up and down the room with hasty strides, and then went away more agitated than displeased. A little while afterwards he came back, saying, "Come to my room, Brockdorf will talk to you about the affair of Elendsheim, and you will see and be convinced that I must have him arrested." I replied, "Very well, I will follow you, and will hear what he has to say, since you wish it."

I did so, and as soon as we entered, the Grand Duke said to Brockdorf, "Speak to the Grand Duchess." Brockdorf, a little confused, bowed to the Duke, and said, "Since your Highness commands me, I will speak to her Imperial Highness the Grand Duchess." Here he paused, and then said, "This is an affair which requires to be managed with much secrecy and prudence." I listened. "All Holstein is full of rumours of the malversations and extortions of Elendsheim. It is true he has no accusers, for he is feared; but when he is arrested, there will be no difficulty in getting as many as may be wished."

I asked for some details of these malversations and extortions, and learnt that as for embezzlement of the revenue, there could not be any, since the Grand Duke had no money in hand there; but what was looked upon as malversation was, that being at the head of the administration of justice, whenever any cause was to be tried, there was always some pleader or other who complained of injustice, and accused the opposite party of having gained their cause by bribing the judges. But M. Brockdorf displayed his eloquence and skill in vain; he did not convince me. I still maintained to him, in presence of the Grand Duke, that they were pushing on his Imperial Highness to commit an act of crying injustice, by persuading him to despatch an order for the arrest of a man against whom there existed no formal complaint or accusation.

I said to M. Brockdorf that after that fashion the Grand Duke might have him locked up at any hour, and say that the crimes and accusations would come afterwards; and that, as to lawsuits, it was easy to conceive that he who lost his cause would always complain of having been wronged. I added, too, that the Grand Duke, more than any other person, ought to be on his guard against such things, as experience had already taught him, to his cost, what persecution and party-spirit could do; for it was not more than two or three years, at the utmost, since his Imperial Highness, at my intercession, had ordered the release of M. de Holmer, who had been kept in prison for six or eight years, in order to compel him to give an account of affairs transacted during the Grand Duke's minority, and under the administration of his guardian, the Prince Royal of Sweden, to whom M. de Holmer had been attached, and whom he followed to Sweden; whence he did not return until the Grand Duke had signed and sent him a testimonial of approval, and a formal discharge for all that had been done during his minority. And yet in spite of all this, the Grand Duke had been induced to have M. de Holmer arrested, and a commission of inquiry appointed, to examine into things which occurred under the administration of the Prince Royal of Sweden. This commission, after acting at first with much vigour, and offering a clear stage to all informers, had, nevertheless, been able to discover nothing, and had fallen into lethargy for want of aliment.

Yet all this time, M. de Holmer languished in close confinement, being allowed to see neither wife, nor children, nor friends, nor relatives; until at last the whole country cried out against the injustice and tyranny of this business, which was in truth outrageous, and which would not even then have been so soon brought to an end had I not advised the Grand Duke to cut this Gordian knot by despatching an order for the release of M. de Holmer, and the abolition of the commission, which, besides, cost no trifling sum to the already nearly exhausted exchequer of the Grand Duke's hereditary duchy. But it was to no purpose that I quoted this striking example; the Grand Duke listened to me, thinking all the while, I fancy, of something else, while M. Brockdorf, hardened in wickedness, narrow in mind, and obstinate as a block, allowed me to talk on, having no more reasons to produce. And when I was gone away, he told the Grand Duke that all I had urged sprung from no other motive than the desire of ruling; that I disapproved of every measure which I had not myself advised; that I knew nothing of business; that women always liked to be meddling in everything, and always spoilt whatever they did meddle with; and that all vigorous measures especially were beyond their capacity; in short, he managed to overrule my advice, and the Grand Duke, at his persuasion, had an order for the arrest of Elendsheim drawn up, signed, and immediately despatched. A person of the name of Zeitz, secretary to the Grand Duke, who was in the interest of Pechlin, and was son-in-law of the midwife who attended me, informed me of all this.

The party of Pechlin, generally, disapproved of this violent and unreasonable measure, with which M. Brockdorf alarmed both them and the whole country of Holstein. As soon as I learnt that the wiles of M. Brockdorf had prevailed over my advice and earnest representations, in a case of such crying injustice, I resolved to make M. Brockdorf feel my indignation to the utmost. I told Zeitz, and I had Pechlin informed, that from that moment I regarded M. Brockdorf as a pest, to be shunned and driven away from the Grand Duke, if it could in any manner be accomplished; as for myself, I would employ every means in my power for that end. And, in fact, I made it a point to manifest, on every occasion, the disgust and the horror with which the conduct of this man had inspired me. There was no sort of ridicule with which he was not covered, and I did not allow any one, whenever an occasion offered, to remain ignorant of what I thought of him.

Leon Narichkine, and other young people, amused themselves in seconding me in this. Whenever M. Brockdorf passed through the apartments, everyone cried out after him, Pelican—such was the nickname we had given him.

This bird was the most hideous that we knew of, and as a man, M. Brockdorf was quite as hideous, both externally and internally. He was tall, with a long neck, and a broad, flat head, and withal red-haired. He wore a wire wig; his eyes were small, dull and sunk in his head, and almost destitute of eyelashes and eyebrows, while the corners of his mouth hung down towards his chin, giving him a miserable as well as an evil look. As to his character I may refer to what I have just said; but I will further add that he was so corrupt that he took money from all who were willing to give it him, and in order that his august master might not at some future time be able to blame these extortions, and seeing him always in need of money, he persuaded him to do the same, and in this way he procured him all he could, as well by selling Holstein orders and titles to any one who would pay for them, as by inducing him to solicit, and intrigue for, in the different bureaux of the empire, as well as in the senate, all sorts of things, many of them unjust, some even burdensome to the state, such as monopolies and other privileges which could not otherwise be allowed, since they were contrary to the laws of Peter I. Besides this, M. Brockdorf led the Duke more than ever into drink and debauchery, having surrounded him with a mob of adventurers, drawn from the barracks and taverns, both of Germany and St. Petersburg, who had neither faith nor principle, and did nothing but drink, eat, smoke, and talk disgusting nonsense.

As I saw that, in spite of all I did and said to lessen the credit of M. Brockdorf, he still maintained his position in the good opinion of the Grand Duke, and was even more in favour than ever, I formed the resolution of telling Count Schouvaloff what I thought of the man, adding, that I looked upon him as one of the most dangerous persons it was possible to have near a young prince, heir to a great empire, and that I felt myself in conscience bound to speak to him in confidence, in order that he might inform the Empress, or take what other measures he might deem proper.

He asked whether he might venture to mention my name. I told him he might, and that if the Empress asked me about it I would not mince the matter, but tell her what I knew and saw. Count Alexander Schouvaloff winked his eye as he listened to me very seriously, but he was not a person to act without the advice of his brother Peter and his cousin Ivan. For a long time I heard nothing; at last he gave me to understand that the Empress might speak to me on the subject.

In the interim, the Grand Duke bounced into my room one day, closely followed by his secretary Zeitz, with a paper in his hand. The Duke, addressing me, said, "Just look at this devil of a fellow! I drank too much yesterday, and to-day my brain is still in a whirl, and he brings me a whole sheet of paper, which, after all, is only a list of the matters which he wishes me to finish; he follows me even into your room." Zeitz said to me, "All that I have got here only requires a yes or a no, and will not take up a quarter of an hour." "Well, let us see," I said, "perhaps you will get through them easier than you think." Zeitz began to read, and as he read on, I answered, 'yes' or 'no.' This pleased the Grand Duke, and Zeitz said to him, "Look, my Lord, if you would only consent to do thus twice a week, your affairs would not fall into arrear. These things are but trifles, but they must be attended to, and the Grand Duchess has finished the matter with six times 'yes,' and as many times 'no.'" Thenceforward his Imperial Highness used to send Zeitz to me whenever he had any "yeses" or "noes." After a time, I asked him to give me a written order, stating what things I might settle, and what I must not determine without his express direction, and this he did. None but Pechlin, Zeitz, and myself were cognizant of this arrangement, with which Pechlin and Zeitz were delighted. When a signature was necessary, the Grand Duke signed what I had settled. The affair of Elendsheim remained under the care of Brockdorf; but when once Elendsheim was under arrest, M. Brockdorf was in no hurry to push the business, for he had thus gained pretty nearly all he wanted, which was to remove Elendsheim from public affairs, and to manifest in Holstein his own influence with his master.

I seized, one day, a favourable opportunity for saying to the Grand Duke, that since he found the affairs of Holstein so troublesome to regulate, and regarded them as a sample of what he would have one day to settle when the Empire of Russia fell to his lot, I thought he must look forward to that charge as something more oppressive still; thereupon he repeated what he had often said to me before—that he felt he was not born for Russia; that he did not suit the Russians nor the Russians him; and that he was persuaded he should perish in Russia. On this point I said to him what I had also said to him many a time before, that he ought not to allow himself to give way to so fatal an idea, but to do his best to make himself liked by every one in Russia, and to ask the Empress to allow him an opportunity of making himself acquainted with the affairs of the empire. I induced him even to ask permission to be present at the conferences which served as a council for the Empress. In fact, he did speak of this to the Schouvaloffs, who induced the Empress to admit him to these conferences whenever she was present at them herself. This was pretty nearly the same thing as settling that he should never be admitted, for after going with him once or twice, neither of them again attended.

The advice which I gave to the Grand Duke was, in general, good and salutary; but he who gives counsel can only do so in accordance with his own cast of mind and turn of thought—his own mode of action and manner of viewing things. But the great object of my counsels to the Grand Duke consisted in the fact that his way of doing things was quite different from mine, and the more we advanced in years the more marked did this difference become.

I made it a point, in all things, to keep as close to truth as I possibly could, while he receded from it farther and farther every day, until at last he became a determined liar. As the way in which he became so is rather singular, I will state it, as it may perhaps display the course of the human mind on this point, and so be useful in showing how this vice may be prevented or corrected in those who may evince a tendency towards it. The first falsehood invented by the Grand Duke was told with a view of giving himself consequence in the eyes of some young married woman or girl, on whose ignorance he could count. He would tell her how, while still living with his father in Holstein, his father had put him at the head of a detachment of his guards and had sent him to seize a troop of gipsies who were prowling about Kiel and committing, he said, frightful robberies. These he would relate in detail, as also the several stratagems he had made use of to surround them and to engage them in one or many battles, in which he pretended to have performed prodigies of skill and valour, after which he had taken them prisoners and carried them to Kiel. At first he took care not to tell all this to any one but those who were ignorant of his history. By degrees he grew bold enough to produce his composition before those on whose discretion he could so far rely as not to fear a contradiction from them; but when he ventured to relate this story to me, I asked him how long before his father's death it had taken place.

He replied, without hesitation, "Three or four years." "Well," I said, "you began very young to show your prowess; for, three or four years before your father's death, you were not more than six or seven years old, having been left, at the age of eleven, under the guardianship of my uncle, the Prince Royal of Sweden. And what equally astonishes me," I observed, "is that your father, of whom you were the only son, and one too whose health, according to what I have been told, was always delicate at that period, should have sent you to fight against brigands, and that too at the early age of six or seven." The Grand Duke became terribly angry at these remarks, saying that I disbelieved him and wished to represent him as a liar in the eyes of the world. I told him it was not I, but the almanac who threw discredit on his story; and that I left it to himself to judge whether it was possible, in the nature of things, that a child of six or seven, an only son, the heir-apparent of a principality, and the only hope of his father, should be sent to catch gipsies.

He held his tongue, and I too; but he sulked with me for a long while. When, however, he had forgotten my remonstrances, he still continued to relate, even in my presence, this story, of which he gave endless variations. He afterwards made up another far more disgraceful, as well as more injurious to himself, which I will relate in its proper place.

It would be impossible for me at present to tell all the dreams which he occasionally imagined and gave out as facts, but in which there was not a shadow of truth. The illustration I have given, will, I think, be sufficient for the present.

One Thursday, towards the end of the Carnival, there being a ball in our apartments, I was sitting between the sister-in-law of Leon Narichkine and his sister, Madame Siniavine, and we were looking at Marine Ossipovna Sakrefskaïa, Maid of Honour to the Empress and niece of the Count Rasoumowsky, who was dancing a minuet. She was at this time slight and active, and it was said that Count Horn was very much in love with her. But as he was always in love with three women at a time, he also paid his addresses to the Countess Marie Romanovna Voronzoff and to Anne Alexievna Hitroff, who were likewise Maids of Honour to her Imperial Majesty. We thought that the first-mentioned danced well, and that she was rather pretty. She was dancing with Leon Narichkine. While talking on this subject, his sister-in-law and sister told me that his mother talked of marrying him to Mademoiselle Hitroff, a niece of the Schouvaloffs, on the side of her mother, who was the sister of Peter and Alexander Schouvaloff, and married to the father of Mademoiselle Hitroff. This gentleman was often at the Narichkines, and had so managed that Leon's mother had conceived the idea of this marriage. Neither Madame Siniavine nor his sister-in-law were at all anxious for a connection with the Schouvaloffs, whom, as I have already said, they did not at all like, and as for Leon, he was not even aware that his mother was thinking of marrying him, while he was actually in love with the Countess Marie Voronzoff just spoken of.

On hearing this, I told Mesdames Siniavine and Narichkine that we must not permit this marriage with Mademoiselle Hitroff, who was a person very much disliked, was intriguing, disagreeable, and boisterous, and that, to cut short all such ideas, we ought to give Leon a wife of our own sort. For this purpose I suggested the above-named niece of the Count Rasoumowsky, a lady of whom, besides, they were both very fond, and who was always at their house.

My two friends greatly approved of my advice, and next day, as there was a masquerade at court, I addressed myself to Marshal Rasoumowsky, who was at that time Hetman of the Ukraine, and told him in plain terms that he was doing very wrong to allow his niece to lose such a desirable husband as Leon Narichkine; that his mother wished him to marry Mademoiselle Hitroff, but that Madame Siniavine, his sister-in-law, and myself, were agreed that his niece would be a more suitable person; and that therefore he ought, without loss of time, to make the proposal to the parties interested.

The Marshal relished our project, spoke of it to his then factotum, Teploff, who at once went and spoke of it to the elder Count Rasoumowsky, who also gave his consent. The very next morning Teploff went to the Bishop of St. Petersburg, and purchased for fifty roubles the necessary dispensation. This being obtained, the Marshal and his wife went to their aunt, the mother of Leon, and managed so well that they gained her consent even against her own wishes.

They were but just in time, for that very day she was to give her decision to M. Hitroff. This being done, Marshal Rasoumowsky, Mesdames Siniavine and Narichkine, broke the matter to Leon, and persuaded him to marry one of whom he had not even had a thought, while he was actually in love with another. She, however, was as good as promised to Count Boutourline. As for Madame Hitroff, he did not care for her at all. This consent being gained, the Marshal sent for his niece, and she felt that the match was too good to be refused. The next day, which was Sunday, the two Counts Rasoumowsky asked the Empress' consent to the match, which she gave at once.

The Schouvaloffs were astonished at the manner in which M. Hitroff and themselves also had been outwitted, for it was not until the consent of the Empress had been obtained that they even heard of the matter. However, the affair being settled, there was no help for it, and thus Leon, in love with one woman, and his mother wishing him to marry another, married a third, of whom neither he nor any one else had thought three days before. This marriage of Leon Narichkine united me still more closely than ever in friendship with the Counts Rasoumowsky, who were really grateful to me for having procured so excellent and so high a match for their niece, nor were they at all sorry at having got the better of the Schouvaloffs, who could not even complain, but were obliged to conceal their mortification. It was, moreover, an additional distinction which I had thus procured for them.

The amours of the Grand Duke with Madame Teploff were now in rather a languishing condition. One of the greatest obstacles in their way was the difficulty of seeing one another, and this vexed his Imperial Highness, who was no fonder of difficulties than he was of answering letters. At the end of the Carnival, his amours began to be a matter of party. The Princess of Courland informed me one day that Count Roman Voronzoff, the father of the two young ladies who were at the court, and who by the way was the horror of the Grand Duke, as were also his five children, was in the habit of speaking of the Grand Duke with very little respect or reserve.

Among other things, he said that if he thought proper he could easily convert the Duke's antipathy into favour, it being only necessary to give a dinner to Brockdorf, let him have plenty of English beer to drink, and when going away, put six bottles of it into his pocket for his Imperial Highness, and then he and his youngest daughter would at once take the highest places in the Grand Duke's favour. At the ball the same evening, I observed a good deal of whispering between his Imperial Highness and the Countess Marie Voronzoff, the eldest daughter of Count Roman, for this family had really become very intimate with the Schouvaloffs, with whom Brockdorf was always welcome. It would have given me anything but pleasure to have seen Mademoiselle Elizabeth Voronzoff come again into favour, and therefore, to put an additional obstacle in the way, I told the Grand Duke what the father had said, and what I have just related. He became almost furious, and demanded in great anger from whom I had heard this. For a long while I was unwilling to tell him, but he said that as I could not name any one, he should believe that I had myself made up this story in order to damage the character of both the father and daughters. It was in vain that I told him I had never in my life made up any such tale; I was obliged at last to name the Princess of Courland. He told me that he should instantly write her a note to London whether I had spoken the truth, and that should there be the least variation between our accounts, he would complain to the Empress of my intrigues and lies; and with these remarks he left the room. Fearing that the answer of the Princess might be in some degree equivocal, I wrote her a note saying, "In Heaven's name, tell the truth purely and simply on the matter which you are going to be asked about." My note was instantly despatched, and reached her in time, for it got before the Grand Duke's. The Princess of Courland gave a truthful answer to his Imperial Highness, and he found that I had not told him a falsehood. This withheld him for some time from his "liaisons" with these two daughters of a man who had but little esteem for him, and whom besides he himself disliked.

But in order to put an additional obstacle in the way, Leon Narichkine persuaded Count Rasoumowsky to invite the Duke to his house one or two evenings each week, quite in private. It was almost a partie quarrée, for no one was present at it but the Marshal, Marie Paolovna Narichkine, the Grand Duke, Madame Teploff, and Leon Narichkine.

This went on for a good part of Lent, and gave rise to another idea. The Marshal's house was at this time of wood. He received company in his wife's apartments, and as they were both fond of play, there was always play there.

The Marshal used to go backwards and forwards, and in his private apartments he had his own coterie, when the Grand Duke was not there. But as the Marshal had often been at my rooms in my little furtive parties, he wished our caterer to come in turn to his home. With this view, what he called his hermitage, which consisted of two or three rooms on the ground-floor, was destined for us. Every one was carefully concealed, because, as I have already said, we dared not go out without permission. By this arrangement there were three or four parties in the house; the Marshal went from one to the other, and mine was the only one that knew all that was going on in the house, whereas none knew that we were there.

Towards the spring M. Pechlin, minister of the Grand Duke for Holstein, died. The Grand Chancellor, Count Bestoujeff, foreseeing his death, had advised me to ask the Grand Duke to give the place to a certain M. Stambke.

At the commencement of spring we went to Oranienbaum. Here our mode of life was the same as in previous years, with this exception, that the number of Holstein troops, and of adventurers who were appointed as officers over them, was augmented year by year; and as it was impossible to find quarters for them in the little village of Oranienbaum, where at the first there were no more than twenty-eight cottages, tents were pitched for these troops, whose number never exceeded 1300 men. The officers dined and supped at court; but as the number of ladies belonging to the court, together with the wives of the gentlemen, did not exceed fifteen or sixteen, and as his Imperial Highness was passionately fond of grand entertainments, which he frequently gave, both in his camp, and in every nook and corner of Oranienbaum, he admitted to these entertainments, not only the female singers and ballet-girls of his opera, but also a great many women of the middle class, of very bad character, who were brought to him from St. Petersburg.

As soon as I was aware that these singing women, etc., were to be admitted, I abstained from attending, under pretext at first that I was taking the waters, and the greater part of the time I took my meals in my own rooms with two or three persons. I afterwards told the Grand Duke that I was afraid the Empress would be displeased if I appeared in so mixed a company; and, in fact, I never went when I knew that the hospitality was general, and therefore, whenever the Grand Duke wished me to come, none were admitted but the ladies of the court. At the masquerades which the Grand Duke gave at Oranienbaum, I never appeared otherwise than very simply dressed, without jewels or ornaments.

This, too, had a good effect with the Empress, who neither liked nor approved of these fêtes at Oranienbaum, which really became orgies; and yet she tolerated them, or at least did not forbid them. I was informed that her Imperial Highness said, "These fêtes give no more pleasure to the Grand Duchess than they do to me; she goes to them dressed in the simplest manner possible, and never sups with the crowd admitted to them." I occupied myself at this time at Oranienbaum in building and planting what is there called my garden, and the rest of the time I took exercise either in walking, riding, or driving, and in my own room I read.

In the month of July we heard that Memel had surrendered on terms to the Russian troops on the 24th of June, and in August the news arrived of the Battle of Gross-Jægersdorf, won by the Russian army on the 19th of that month.

On the day of the Te Deum, I gave a grand entertainment in my garden to the Grand Duke, and to all the most distinguished people at Oranienbaum, at which the Grand Duke and all the company appeared very gay, and very much pleased. This diminished for the moment the pain which the Grand Duke felt at the war which had just broken out between Russia and the King of Prussia, for which ever since his boyhood he had felt a singular inclination.

This at the first was natural enough, but in the end it degenerated into madness. At this time the public joy at the success of the arms of Russia obliged him to dissemble his real sentiments, which were that he saw with regret the defeat of the Prussian troops, which he regarded as invincible. On that day I had an ox roasted for the masons and laborers at Oranienbaum.

A few days after this entertainment we returned to the capital, where we occupied the Summer Palace.

Here Count Alexander Schouvaloff came one evening to tell me that the Empress was in his wife's room, and that she had sent word to me to come there and speak to her, as I had desired last winter. I went without delay to the apartment of the Count and Countess Schouvaloff, which was at the end of my own apartments, and found the Empress there quite alone. After kissing her hand and receiving her embrace in return, she did me the honour to say, that having been informed that I wanted to speak to her, she had come to-day to know what it was I wanted. It was now eight months and more since my conversation with Alexander Schouvaloff on the subject of Brockdorf. I replied to her Imperial Majesty that last winter, seeing the way in which M. Brockdorf acted, I had thought it necessary to speak of it to Count Alexander Schouvaloff, in order that he might apprise her Imperial Majesty of it; that he had asked if he might name me as his authority, and that I had told him that, if her Imperial Majesty wished it, I would repeat to her all that I knew.

Thereupon I related the story of Elendsheim as it had taken place. She seemed to listen to me very coldly, then she asked me for details of the private life of the Grand Duke and of his associates. I told her with the greatest truth all that I knew of them, and when, with regard to the affairs of Holstein, I entered into some details which showed her that I was well acquainted with them, she said to me, "You seem to be well informed in regard to that country."

I said very simply that that was not a difficulty, as the Grand Duke had ordered me to make myself acquainted with them. I saw from her countenance that this confidence made a disagreeable impression on her mind, and generally she appeared to me unusually close during this conversation, in which she questioned me, and made me talk, scarcely saying a word herself, so that this interview appeared to me rather a kind of inquisition on her part, than a confidential conversation. At last she dismissed me quite as coldly as she received me, and I was very little pleased with my audience, which Alexander Schouvaloff recommended me to keep quite secret, which I promised him to do, and indeed there was nothing in it to boast of. On my return I attributed the coldness of the Empress to the antipathy with which, as I had long been informed, the Schouvaloffs had inspired her against me. It will be seen as we proceed what a detestable use, if I may venture to say so, they persuaded her to make of the private conversation.

Some time after this we learned that Marshal Apraxine, far from profiting by his success after the capture of Memel and the victory of Gross-Jægersdorf, to push onwards, was retiring with such precipitation, that his retreat resembled a flight, for he threw away or burned his carriages and spiked his guns. No one understood these operations: his friends, even, could not justify him, and on that account it was suspected that there must be some foul play.

Although I do not myself know to what exactly to attribute the precipitate and inconsistent retreat of Marshal Apraxine, never having seen him since, yet I think the cause of it may have been that he received from his daughter, the Princess Kourakine, always connected by policy, though not by inclination, with Peter Schouvaloff, from his son-in-law, Prince Kourakine, and from his friends and relatives, very precise news of the health of the Empress, which was constantly getting worse and worse. At this time it began generally to be conceived that she had very violent convulsions every month, regularly; that these convulsions visibly enfeebled her faculties; that after every convulsion she was for three or four days in a state of weakness and exhaustion which resembled lethargy; and that during this period she could not be spoken to on any subject whatsoever. Marshal Apraxine, perhaps thinking the danger more urgent than it really was, did not judge it advisable to advance farther into Prussia, but thought it best to make a retrograde movement, in order to draw nearer to the frontiers of Russia, under pretext of want of provisions, foreseeing that, in the event of the Empress' death, the war would be brought at once to a close. It was difficult to justify the proceedings of Marshal Apraxine.

But such may have been his views, and the more so as he believed his presence necessary in Russia, as I have already mentioned, when speaking of his departure. Count Bestoujeff informed me, through Stambke, of the turn which the conduct of Marshal Apraxine had taken, and how the Imperial Ambassador, and that of France, loudly complained of it. He begged me to write to the Marshal, as being his friend, and join my persuasions to his, to induce him to retrace his steps and put an end to a flight to which his enemies gave an odious and injurious interpretation. I did write to him, and informed him of the reports current at St. Petersburg, and of the difficulty which his friends found in justifying the precipitancy of his retreat, and begged him to retrace his steps and fulfil the orders he had received from the Government. This letter was sent to him through Bestoujeff, but I received no reply to it. Meanwhile General Fermor, Director-General of Works to her Imperial Majesty, came to take leave of us on his departure from St. Petersburg. We learned that he was appointed to the army. He had formerly been Quarter-master-general to Count Munich. The first thing which he asked for was to have with him his employés or superintendents, at the board of works, the Brigadiers Reaznoff and Mordvinoff; and with them he set off for the army. These were soldiers who had scarcely ever done anything but make contracts for building. On his arrival he was ordered to take the command, in place of Marshal Apraxine, who was recalled, and who, on his return, found at Trihorsky an order to await there the commands of the Empress.

These were long in reaching him, because his friends, his daughter, and Peter Schouvaloff moved heaven and earth to calm the anger of the Empress, fomented as it was by Counts Voronzoff, Boutourline, John Schouvaloff, and others, who were urged on by the ambassadors of the courts of Vienna and Versailles, who were anxious to have the Marshal brought to trial. At last, commissioners were named to examine him. After the first interrogatory, the Marshal was seized with a fit of apoplexy, of which he died in about twenty-four hours. In this trial, General Lieven would assuredly have also been included. He was the friend and confidant of Apraxine. I should have had an additional grief, for Lieven was sincerely attached to me. But whatever friendship I may have had for Apraxine and Lieven, I can swear that I was entirely ignorant of the cause of their conduct, and even of their conduct itself, although a good deal of trouble was taken to circulate a report that it was to please the Grand Duke and me that they had retreated instead of advancing. Lieven occasionally gave very singular proofs of his attachment to me; among others, the following. The Ambassador of Austria, Count Esterhazy, gave a masquerade, at which the Empress and all the court were present. Lieven, seeing me pass the room where he was, said to his neighbour, who was Count Poniatowsky, "There is a woman for whom a fellow might take some blows of the knout without complaining." I have this anecdote from Count Poniatowsky himself, since King of Poland.

## 1758

As soon as General Fermor had assumed the command, he hastened to fulfil his instructions, which were precise. He instantly moved forward, in spite of the rigour of the season, and occupied Königsberg, which sent deputies to him on

18th January, 1758.

During this winter I suddenly perceived a great change in the behaviour of Leon Narichkine. He began to be disrespectful and rude; no longer visited me except unwillingly, and talked in a manner which made it evident that some one was filling his head with prejudices against me, his sister-in-law, his sister, Count Poniatowsky, and all who held to me.

I learned that he was constantly at the house of John Schouvaloff, and I easily guessed that they were turning him against me, in order to punish me for having prevented his marriage with Mademoiselle Hitroff, and that they would certainly go on until they had led him into indiscretions which might be injurious to me. His sister-in-law, his sister, and his brother were equally angry with him on my account, and, literally, he conducted himself like a fool, and took delight in offending us as much as he could, and that, too, while I was furnishing, at my own expense, the house in which he was to live when married. Every one accused him of ingratitude, and told him that he had no interest in what he was doing; in a word, that he had nothing whatever to complain of. It was evident that he was a mere tool in the hands of those who had got possession of him. He was more regular in paying court to the Grand Duke, whom he amused as much as he could, leading him on more and more to courses which he knew I disapproved of. He sometimes pushed his incivility so far as not to reply when I spoke to him. To this very hour I cannot conceive what could have offended him, for I had literally loaded him with favours and friendship, as also all his family, from the first moment I knew them.

I fancy he was also induced to cajole the Grand Duke, by the advice of the Schouvaloffs, who told him that the Duke's favour would be more advantageous than mine, since I was in ill odour both with him and the Empress, neither of whom liked me, and that he would interfere with his own prospects if he did not detach himself from me; that as soon as the Empress died, the Grand Duke would put me into a convent; and other such like statements which the Schouvaloffs made to him, and which were reported to me. Besides, they showed him in perspective the order of St. Anne as the symbol of the Grand Duke's favour. By these and such like reasonings and promises, they obtained from this weak-minded young man, all the little treacheries they wished; indeed, they made him go not only as far, but even farther than they wished, although now and then, as will hereafter be seen, he had his fits of repentance.

He also endeavoured, as much as possible, to alienate the Grand Duke from me, so that his Imperial Highness manifested an almost continuous ill-humour towards me, while he again renewed his connection with the Countess Elizabeth Voronzoff.

In the beginning of the spring of this year it was rumoured that Prince Charles of Saxony, son of Augustus III, King of Poland, intended to visit St. Petersburg. The prospect of this visit appeared no pleasure to the Grand Duke, for many reasons. In the first place, he feared that it would be an additional restraint upon him, as he did not like that the course of life which he had traced out for himself should be in the least disturbed.

In the next place the house of Saxony stood opposed to the King of Prussia, while a third reason may have been that he feared to suffer by comparison; if so, this, at all events, was being very modest, for the poor Prince of Saxony was a mere nonentity and wholly devoid of education. Except hunting and dancing, he knew absolutely nothing, and he told me himself that in the whole course of his life he never had a book in his hand except the prayer-books given to him by his mother, who was a great bigot. The Prince, in short, arrived at St. Petersburg on the 5th of April, in this year.

He was received with much ceremony, and a great display of magnificence and splendour. His suite was very numerous, and he was accompanied by many Poles and Saxons, among whom there was a Lubomirsky, a Pototsky, a Rzevusky, who enjoyed the appellation of "the handsome," two princes, Soulkowsky, a Count Sapieha, the Count Branitsky, since Grand-General, a Count Einsiedel, and many others, whose names do not now occur to me. He had a kind of sub-governor or tutor with him, named Lachinal, who directed his conduct and his correspondence.

The Prince took up his residence in the house of the chamberlain, John Schouvaloff, which was recently finished, and on which its owner had exhausted his taste, notwithstanding which the house was tasteless and inconveniently though richly furnished. There were numerous paintings, but the greater part were only copies. One of the rooms was ornamented with tchinar wood, but as this wood does not take a polish it had been varnished; this turned it yellow, but of a very disagreeable hue, and, this being pronounced ugly, they sought to remedy it by covering it with very elaborate carvings, which they silvered. Externally, this mansion, though imposing in itself, resembled in its decorations, ruffles of Alençon lace, so loaded was it with ornament. Count John Czernickeff was appointed to attend on Prince Charles, and the Prince was provided with everything he required at the expense of the court, and waited on by the servants of the court.

The night preceding the day of Prince Charles's visit to us, I suffered so severely from a violent attack of cholic, with such looseness of the bowels that they were moved more than thirty times. Notwithstanding this, and the fever consequent

*Catherine 2nd on a balcony of the Winter Palace on 28 June 1762, the day of the coup*

upon it, I dressed the next morning to receive the Prince of Saxony. He was presented to the Empress about two o'clock in the afternoon, and, upon leaving her, was presented to me. The Grand Duke was to enter a moment after him.

Three arm-chairs had been placed side by side along the same wall, the centre one was for me, that on my right for the Grand Duke, and the one on my left for the Prince of Saxony. The task of keeping up the conversation devolved entirely upon me, for the Grand Duke had hardly a word to say, and the Prince had no conversational powers. In short, after a brief interview of a quarter of an hour's length, Prince Charles arose to present his immense suite to us.

There were with him, I think, more than twenty persons, to whom were added, upon this occasion, the Polish and Saxon Envoys who resided at the Russian Court, together with their employés. After half an hour's interview the Prince took leave, and I undressed and went to bed, where I remained three or four days in a very violent fever, at the end of which I showed some signs of pregnancy. At the end of April we went to Oranienbaum. Before our departure we learnt that Prince Charles of Saxony intended to join the Russian army as a volunteer. Before leaving for the army, he went with the Empress to Petershoff where he was fêted. We took no part in these festivities, or in those given in the capital, but remained at our country-house, where he came to take leave of us, and then departed on the 4th of July.

As the Grand Duke was almost always in very bad humour with me, for which I could find no other reasons than my not receiving either M. Brockdorf or the Countess Voronzoff, who again was becoming the reigning favourite, it occurred to me to give a fête to his Imperial Highness in my garden at Oranienbaum, in order, if possible, to mitigate this ill-feeling. A fête was a thing always welcome to his Imperial Highness. Accordingly, I ordered an Italian architect who was at that time in my service, Antonio Renaldi, to construct, in a retired spot in the wood a large car capable of containing an orchestra of sixty persons, singers and instrumentalists. I had verses composed by the Italian poet of the court, and set to music by the chapel-master, Araja. In the large avenue of the garden was placed an illuminated decoration with a curtain, opposite to which a table was laid out for supper. On the 17th of July, at the close of day, his Imperial Highness, and all who were at Oranienbaum and numerous spectators from St. Petersburg and Cronstadt, assembled in the gardens which they found illuminated. We sat down to table, and, after the first course, the curtain which concealed the grand avenue was raised, and in the distance the ambulatory orchestra was seen approaching, drawn by twenty oxen, decorated with garlands and surrounded by all the dancers, male and female, that I had been able to get together.

The avenue was illuminated, and so bright that everything could be plainly distinguished. When the car stopped, it so happened that the moon stood directly over it—a circumstance which produced an admirable effect and took the company quite by surprise; the weather, besides, was most delightful. The guests sprang from table, and advanced nearer to enjoy more fully the beauty of the symphony and of the spectacle. When this was ended the curtain dropped, and we sat down again to table for the second course; after which a flourish of trumpets and cymbals was heard, and then a mountebank cried out, "This way, ladies and gentlemen; walk in here, and you will find lottery tickets for nothing."

At each side of the curtained decoration two small curtains were now raised, displaying two small shops brightly illuminated, at one of which tickets were distributed gratis for a lottery of the porcelain it contained; and, in the other, for flowers, fans, combs, purses, ribbons, gloves, sword-knots, and other similar trifles. When the stalls were empty dessert was served, and afterwards came dancing, which was kept up till six the next morning. For once in the way, no intrigue or ill-will occurred to mar the effect of my fête, and his Imperial Highness and every one besides was in ecstasies. Nothing was to be heard but laudations of the Grand Duchess and her fête; and, indeed, I had spared no expense.

My wine was pronounced delicious; the repast the best possible. All was at my own expense, and cost from 10,000 to 15,000 roubles; it must be remembered that I had 30,000 roubles a-year. But this fête was near costing me still more dearly; for, during the day of the 17th of July, having gone in a cabriolet with Madame Narichkine to see the preparations, and wishing to descend from the carriage, just as I placed my foot on the step, a sudden movement of the horse threw me on my knees on the ground. I was then four or five months advanced in pregnancy. I pretended to make light of the accident, and remained the last at the fête, doing the honours. However I was very much afraid of a miscarriage, but no ill result occurred, and I escaped with nothing worse than the fright.

The Grand Duke, and all his coterie, all his Holstein retainers, and even my most rancorous enemies, for days afterwards, were never tired of singing my praises, and those of my fête, there being no one, either friend or foe, who did not carry off some trifle or other, as a souvenir; and as at the fête, which was a masquerade, there was a numerous assemblage of all ranks, and as the company in the garden was very mixed, and as among them were a number of women who could not elsewhere have appeared at court, or in my presence, all made a boast and display of my presents, which were, in reality, mere trifles, none of them, I believe, exceeding a hundred roubles in value; but they came from me, and every one was delighted to be able to say, "I received that from her Imperial Highness the Grand Duchess; she is goodness itself; she has made presents to every one; she is charming; she gave me a kind smile, and took pleasure in making us all eat, dance, and divert ourselves; she was always ready to find a place for those who had none, and wished every one to see all that was to be seen. She was very lively," etc.

In short, on that day I was found to possess qualities which had not before been recognized, and I disarmed my enemies. This was what I wanted; but it did not last long, as will shortly appear.

After this fête, Leon Narichkine renewed his visits to me. One day, on entering my boudoir, I found him impertinently stretched on a couch which was there, and singing an absurd song; seeing this, I went out, closing the door after me, and immediately went in search of his sister-in-law, whom I told that we must get a good bundle of nettles, and with them chastise this fellow, who had for some time past behaved so insolently towards us, and teach him to respect us.

His sister-in-law readily consented, and we forthwith had brought to us some good strong rods, surrounded with nettles. We took along with us a widow, who was with me, among my women, by name Tatiana Jourievna, and we all three entered the cabinet, where we found Leon Narichkine singing his song at the top of his voice. When he saw us he tried to make off, but we whipped him so well with our rods and nettles, that his hands, legs, and face were swollen for two or three days to such a degree that he could not accompany us to Peterhoff on the morrow, which was a court day, but was obliged to remain in his room. He took care, besides, not to boast of what had occurred, because we assured him that on the least sign of impoliteness, or ground of complaint from him, we would renew the operation, seeing that there was no other means of managing him. All this was done as mere joke, and without anger, but our hero felt it sufficiently to recollect it, and did not again expose himself to it, at least, not to the same extent as before.

In the month of August, while at Oranienbaum, we learnt that the battle of Zorndorff, one of the most sanguinary of the century, had been fought on the 14th of that month. The number of killed and wounded, on each side, was calculated at upwards of 20,000. Our loss in officers was considerable, and exceeded 1,200. This battle was announced to us as a victory, but it was whispered that the loss was equal on both sides; that for the space of three days neither army ventured to claim the victory; that finally, on the third day, the King of Prussia, in his camp, and the Count Fermor on the field of battle, had each caused the Te Deum to be sung. The vexation of the Empress and the consternation of the city were extreme when they learned all the details of this bloody day, in which so many people lost relatives, friends, or acquaintances. For a long time all was sorrow; a great many generals were slain or wounded or taken prisoners.

At last, it was acknowledged, that the conduct of Count Fermor was anything but soldierly and skilful. He was recalled, and the command of the Russian forces in Prussia was given to Count Peter Soltikoff. For this purpose he was summoned from the Ukraine, where he commanded, and in the interim the command of the army was given to General Froloff Bagreeff, but with secret instructions to do nothing without the concurrence of the Lieutenant-Generals Count Roumianzoff and Prince Alexander Galitzine, his brother-in-law. A charge was brought, to the effect that Fermor, being at no great distance from the field of battle, with a force of 10,000 men upon the heights, whence he could hear the cannonade, might have rendered the action more decisive, had he attacked the Prussian army in the rear while engaged with ours. He neglected to do this, and when his brother-in-law, Prince Galitzine, came to his camp after the battle, and detailed the butchery that had taken place, he received him very ill, said many disagreeable things to him, and refused to see him afterwards, treating him as a coward, which Prince Galitzine by no means was, the entire army being more convinced of his intrepidity than of that of Roumianzoff, notwithstanding his present glory and victories.

At the beginning of September the Empress was at Zarskoe Selo, where, on the 8th of the month, the day of the Nativity of the Blessed Virgin, she went on foot from the palace to the parish church to hear mass, the distance being only a few steps towards the north from the palace-door to the church. Scarcely had the service commenced, when, feeling unwell, she left the church, and descended the little flight of steps which turns towards the palace, and, on arriving at the re-entering angle of the side of the church, she fell down insensible on the grass, in the midst of, or rather surrounded by, a crowd of people who had come to hear mass from all the neighbouring villages.

None of her attendants had followed her when she left the church; but being soon apprised of her condition, the ladies of her suite, and her other intimate attendants, ran to her assistance, and found her without consciousness or movement in the midst of the crowd, who gazed upon her without daring to approach. The Empress was tall and powerful, and could not fall down suddenly without doing herself a good deal of injury by the mere fall. They covered her with a white handkerchief, and went to fetch the physician and surgeon. The latter arrived first, and instantly bled her, just as she lay on the ground, and in the presence of all the crowd. But this did not bring her to. The physician was a long time in coming, being himself ill, and unable to walk. He was obliged to be carried in an arm-chair.

The physician was the late Condoijdij, a Greek by nation, and the surgeon, Fouzadier, a French refugee.

At last screens were brought from the palace as well as a couch, on which she was placed, and by dint of care, and the remedies applied, she began to revive a little; but, on opening her eyes, she recognized no one, and asked, in a scarcely intelligible manner, where she was. All this lasted above two hours, at the end of which it was determined to carry her Majesty on the couch to the palace. The consternation into which this event threw all who were attached to the court may easily be imagined. The publicity of the affair added to its unpleasantness. Hitherto the state of the Empress had been kept very secret, but in this case the accident was public. The next morning I was informed of the event at Oranienbaum by a note from Count Poniatowsky. I immediately went and told the Grand Duke, who knew nothing of it; because, generally speaking, every thing was carefully concealed from us, and more especially all that concerned the Empress herself. Only that it was customary, whenever we happened not to be in the same place as her Majesty, to send every Sunday one of the gentlemen of our court to make inquiries after her health. This we did not fail to do on the following Sunday, and we learnt that for several days the Empress had not recovered the free use of speech, and that even yet she articulated with difficulty. It was asserted that during her swoon she had bitten her tongue. All this gave reason for supposing that this weakness partook more of the nature of convulsions than mere fainting.

At the end of September we returned to the capital, and as I began to get large, I no longer appeared in public, believing that the period of my confinement was much nearer than it really proved to be.

This was a source of annoyance to the Grand Duke, because, when I appeared in public, he very often complained of indisposition, in order to be able to remain in his own apartments, and, as the Empress also rarely appeared, the burden of the reception days, the fêtes, and the balls of the court devolved upon me, and when I could not be there, his Imperial

Highness was teased to be present, in order that some one might represent her Majesty. He, therefore, began to be annoyed at my pregnancy, and one day took it in his head to say, in his apartment, before Leon Narichkine, and several others, "God knows where my wife gets her pregnancies, I don't very well know whether this child is mine, and whether I ought to take the responsibility of it." Leon Narichkine came running to me with these words, fresh from the Duke's lips. I was naturally enough alarmed at such a speech, and said to him, "How stupid you all are.

Go and ask him to swear that he has not slept with his wife, and tell him if he will take this oath, you will go immediately and give information of it to Alexander Schouvaloff as grand inquisitor of the empire." Leon actually went to his Imperial Highness, and asked him for this oath, but the answer he got was, "Go to the devil, and don't talk to me any more about that." This speech of the Grand Duke, made so indiscreetly, gave me great pain, and I saw from that moment that three paths almost equally perilous presented themselves for my choice: first, to share the fortunes of the Grand Duke, be they what they might; secondly, to be exposed every moment to everything he chose to do either for or against me; or, lastly, to take a path entirely independent of all eventualities; to speak more plainly, I had to choose the alternative of perishing with him, or by him, or to save myself, my children, and perhaps the empire also, from the wreck of which all the moral and physical qualities of this Prince made me foresee the danger. This last choice appeared to me the safest.

I resolved, therefore, to the utmost of my power to continue to give him on all occasions the very best advice I could for his benefit, but never to persist in this, as I had hitherto done, so as to make him angry; to open his eyes to his true interests on every opportunity that presented itself; and, during the rest of the time, to maintain a gloomy silence; and, on the other hand, to take care of my own interests with the public, so that in the time of need they might see in me the saviour of the commonwealth. In the month of October I was informed by the High Chancellor, Count Bestoujeff, that the King of Poland had just sent Count Poniatowsky his letters of recall. Count Bestoujeff had had a violent dispute upon this subject with Count Brühl and the Cabinet of Saxony, and was annoyed that he had not been consulted in the matter as heretofore. He learned at last that the Vice-Chancellor, Count Voronzoff, and John Schouvaloff had, with the assistance of Prasse, the resident minister of Saxony, secretly manœuvred the whole affair.

This M. Prasse, moreover, often appeared to be well informed of a number of secrets which it puzzled every one to conjecture whence he had obtained them. Many years afterwards their source was discovered. He carried on a love intrigue, though very secretly and very discreetly, with the Vice-Chancellor's wife, the Countess Anna Karlovna, whose maiden name was Scavronsky. This lady was the intimate friend of the wife of Samarine, the master of the ceremonies, and it was at the house of the latter that the Countess saw M. Prasse. The Chancellor Bestoujeff had all the letters of recall brought to him, and sent them back to Saxony under pretext of informality.

In the night between the 8th and 9th of December, I began to feel the pains of childbirth. I sent to inform the Grand Duke by Madame Vladislava, and also Count Schouvaloff, that he might announce the fact to her Imperial Majesty.

In a short time the Grand Duke came into my room, dressed in his Holstein uniform, booted and spurred, with his scarf round his body, and an enormous sword at his side, having made an elaborate toilet. It was about half-past two in the morning. Astonished at his appearance, I inquired the reason of this grand dress. He replied that it was only on an emergency that true friends could be discerned; that in this garb he was ready to act as duty demanded; that the duty of a Holstein officer was to defend, according to his oath, the ducal palace against all its enemies, and that as I was ill he had hastened to my assistance. One would have supposed him jesting; but not at all, he was quite serious. I saw at once that he was intoxicated, and advised him to go to bed, that the Empress when she came might not have the double annoyance of seeing him in such a state, and armed cap-a-pie in the Holstein uniform, which I knew she detested. I had great difficulty in getting him to leave; however, Madame Vladislava and myself finally persuaded him, with the help of the midwife, who assured him that I should not be delivered for some time yet. At length he went away, and the Empress arrived.

She asked where the Grand Duke was, and she was informed that he had just quitted the room, and would not fail to return. When she found that the pains abated, and that the midwife told her I might not be confined for some hours yet, she returned to her apartments, and I went to bed and slept till the next morning, when I got up as usual, feeling however occasional pains, after which I continued for hours together entirely free from them. Towards supper time I felt hungry, and ordered some supper to be brought. The midwife was sitting near me, and seeing me eat ravenously, she said, "Eat, eat: this supper will bring you good luck." In fact, having finished my supper, I rose from the table, and the moment I did so was seized with such a pain, that I gave a loud scream. The midwife and Madame Vladislava seized me under my arms, and placed me on the "bed of pain," and went to seek the Empress and the Grand Duke.

Scarcely had they arrived when I was delivered (between ten and eleven o'clock at night), on the 9th of December, of a daughter, whom I begged the Empress to allow me to name after her. But she decided that she should be named after her eldest sister, Anne Petrovna, Duchess of Holstein, mother of the Grand Duke. His Imperial Highness appeared much pleased at the birth of this child; he made great rejoicings over it in his own apartments, ordered rejoicings to be made in Holstein also, and received all the compliments paid to him on the subject with great manifestations of pleasure.

On the sixth day the Empress stood godmother to the child, and brought me an order on the cabinet for 60,000 roubles. A similar present was sent to the Grand Duke, which added not a little to his satisfaction. After the baptism the fêtes commenced, which were very magnificent, according to report. I saw none of them, but remained in my bed, very delicate and quite alone, not a living soul to keep me company; for no sooner was I delivered than the Empress not only carried off the child to her own apartments as previously, but under the plea of my requiring repose, I was left there and abandoned like any poor wretch, no one entering my apartments to ask how I was, or even sending to inquire.

As on the former occasion, I had suffered a great deal from this neglect. I had this time taken all possible precautions against draughts, and the other inconveniences of the place; and as soon as I was delivered I arose and went to my bed, and as no one dared to visit me, unless secretly, I had also taken care to provide for this contingency. My bed stood nearly in the middle of a rather long room, the windows being on the right side of the bed. There was also a side door, which opened into a kind of wardrobe, which served also as an ante-chamber, and which was well barricaded with screens and trunks. From the bed to this door I had placed an immense screen which concealed the prettiest little boudoir I could devise, considering the locality and the circumstances. In this boudoir were a couch, mirrors, moveable tables, and some chairs. When the curtains of my bed on that side were drawn, nothing could be seen; but when they were pulled aside, I could see the boudoir, and those who happened to be in it. But any one entering the room could only see the screens. If any one asked what was behind the screen, the answer was, the commode; and this being within the screen, no one was anxious to see it; or even if so, it could be shown without getting into the boudoir, which the screen effectively concealed.

(Continue on the fourth volume)

РИСУНКИ

ОДЕЖДЫ и ВООРУЖЕНІЯ

РОССІЙСКИХЪ

ВОЙСКЪ.

# PLATES LIST OF ILLUSTRATIONS

754. Parade shabraque of the cavaliers, from 1764 to 1796.

755. Ceremonial: portupeya, ljadunka and    shoulder belt of the cavalry guards from 1764 to 1796

756. Guard cavalry helmet from 1764 to 1796

757. Guard cavalry helmet from 1764 to 1796

758. Guard cavalry from 1764 to 1796

759. Private and Trumpet of the leib-hussar squadron, from 1776 to 1796

760. Colonel of the leib-hussar squadron, from 1776 to 1796

761. Private of the leib-hussar squadron, from 1776 to 1796

762. Officer and a Private Chuguevskaya cossack convoy command, from 1776 to 1790

763. Radovoy Chuguevskaya convoy cossack team, from 1776 to 1790

764. NCO and the Private Don cossack convoy, from 1776 to 1790

765. Officer of the Don cossack convoy, from 1776 to 1790

766. Officer of  Don cossack command, from 1776 to 1790

767. Private and Officer of the Convoy cossack teams, 1790-1796

768. Cadet of the 1st Age of the Land Cadet Corps, 1767-1796

769. Cadets of the 3rd and 2nd ages of the Land Cadet Corps, 1767-1796

770. Cadets of the Land Cadet Corps, from 1767 to 1786

771. Cadets of the Land Cadet Corps, from 1767 to 1786

772. Officers of the Land Cadet Corps, 1767-1786

773. Cadet of the 4th and 5th ages of the Land Cadet Corps, from 1767-1786

774. Cadets of the 3rd age of the Land Cadet Corps

775. Officer and 5th-year Cadet of the Land Cadet Corps, from 1786-1796

776. Baraban of the Land Cadet Corps, 1786-1796

777. Cadets of the Artillery and Engineering Cadet Corps, 1762-1784

778. Cadets of the Artillery and Engineering Cadet Corps, 1762-1784

779. Bombardir Jaws Cadet of the Artillery, 1762-1796

780. Engineering Cadet Corps, 1762-1796

781. Officers of the Artillery and Engineering Cadet Corps, 1762-1784

782. Cadet of the Artillery and Engineering Cadet Corps, 1784-1796

783. Pupil of the School of Art at the Artillery and Engineering Cadet Corps, 1762-1784

784. Pupil of the School of Art at the Artillery and Engineering Cadet Corps, 1762-1784

785. Cadet and Officer of the Artillery and Engineering Cadet Corps, 1784-1786

786. Cadet and Officer of the Artillery and Engineering Cadet Corps, 1784-1786

787. Cadets of the Artillery and Engineering Cadet Corps, 1784-1796

788. Officer and Cadet of the Artillery and Engineering Cadet Corps, 1786-1796

789. Ukrainian hussar regiment, from 1776 to 1783

790. Officer of the Gymnasium of the Migrant Mutantners, 1775-1786

791. Vospitannik and Officer of the Gymnasium of the Stranger Mutual believers, 1786-1792

792. Vospitannik Corps of the Migrant Migrant, 1792-1796

793. Officer of the Corps of the Migrant Migrants, 1792-1796

794. Vospitannik Corps of the Stranger Migrant, 1793-1796

795. Veterans of Garrison Battalion, from 1764 to 1786

796. Masterovo Garrison Battalion, from 1764 to 1786

797. Picture of the Garrison Battalion, 1764-1786

798. Garrison General officers, 1764-1780

799. Garrison General Mayor and Garrison Brigadier, 1764-1780

*Officer and NCO of field artillery, from 1769 to 1786*

*Artilleries general from 1780 to 1796*

*Fusilier regiment, from 1786 to 1796*

*Private and NCO of fusilier regiment, from 1786 to 1796*

*Officer of the artillery regiments from 1786 to 1796*

*Garrison artillery of the field artillery, from 1786 to 1796*

*Artillery Officers garrison from 1786 to 1796*

*Private cavalry artillery, from 1794 to 1796*

*Horse-artillery hat, from 1794 to 1796*

*Horse artillery from 1794 to 1796*

*Officer of the horse artillery, from 1794 to 1796*

*Officer, pioneer and miner of the engineering corps, from 1763 to 1786*

*Miner shapka, from 1763 to 1786*

*Private and Officer miner and pioneer's mouth, from 1786 to 1796*

*Officers of the general hospital: general quartermaster-lieutenant, ober-quartermaster and colonial Officer, from 1764 to 1786*

*General-qualified master from 1764 to 1780*

*Arrived to the columns in 1771 and 1772*

*Private and sergeant of the pioneer battalion, from 1771 to 1775*

*NCO pioneer battalion, from 1771 to 1775*

*Officer of the pioneer battalion, from 1771 to 1775*

*Variant to the columns, from 1772 to 1786*

*Officer of the general staff, from 1786 to 1796*

*Private and sergeant musketeers of the regiments of the life guards:*        *Preobrazhensky, Semenovsky and Izmailovsky, from*

*1763 to 1786*

*Fourier badges of regiments of life guards: Preobrazhensky, Semenovsky and Izmailovsky, in 1773*

*Bombardier of the life guards of the Preobrazhensky regiment, from 1763 to 1786*

*Musketeer guardian Officer, from 1763 to 1786*

*Grenadiers of the leb-guardian shelves: Preobrazhensky, Semenovsky and*       *Izmailovsky from 1763 to 1786*

*Shapka of guard grenadier, from 1763 to 1796*

*Guard grenadier Officer, from 1763 to 1786*

*Grenadiers shapka guards Officers, from 1763 to 1796*

*Dragons of life guards: Preobrazhensky, Semenovsky and Izmailovsky, from 1763 to 1786*

*Private of Preobrazhensky regiment, from 1763 to 1786*

*Dragons of the crowns of life guards: Preobrazhensky, Semenovsky and Izmailovsky from 1763 to 1786*

*Musicians of life guards: Preobrazhensky, Semenovsky and Izmailovsky, from 1763 to 1786*

*Guards of Preobrazhensky, Semenovsky and Izmailovsky, from 1763 to 1786*

*Jager polkov life guards: Preobrazhensky, Semenovsky and Izmailovsky, from 1770 to 1786*

*Guard jager Officer, from 1770 to 1786*

*Guardian soldiers, 1773*

*Officer and Private life guards: Preobrazhensky, Semenovsky and Izmailovsky from 1786 to 1796*

*Jagers polkov life guards: Preobrazhensky, Semenovsky and Izmailovsky from 1786 to 1796*

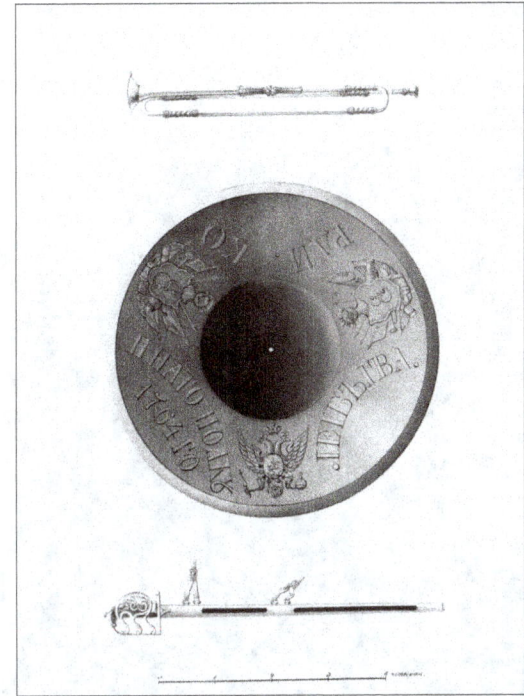

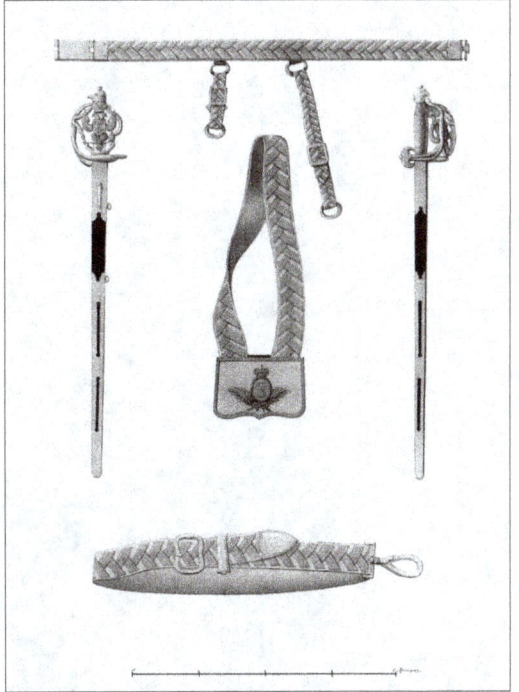

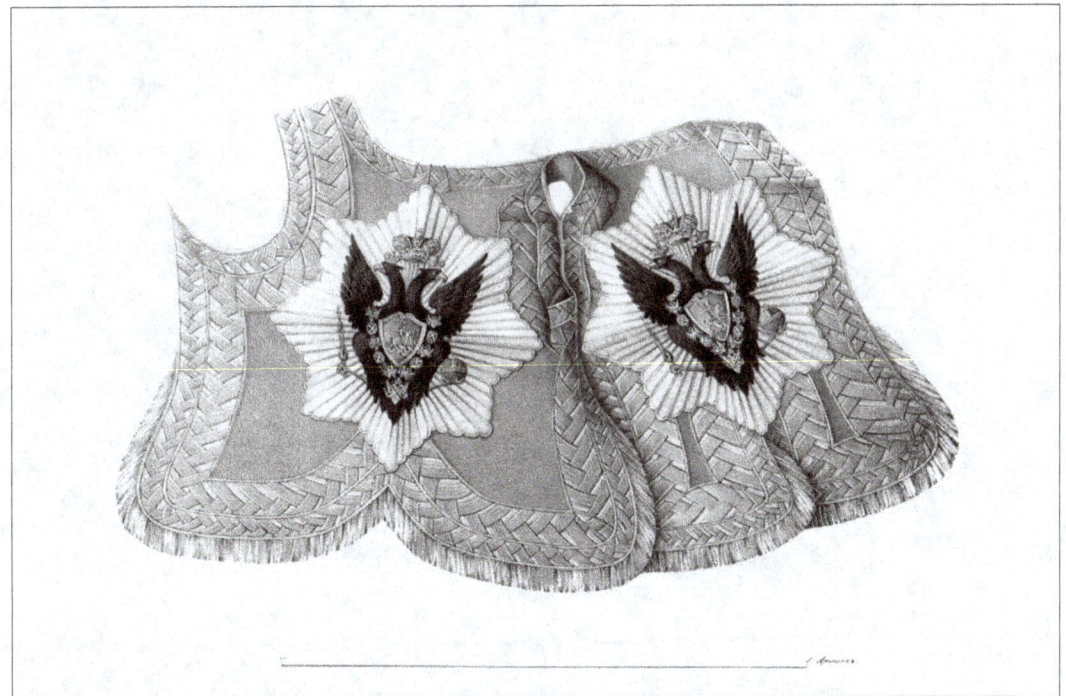

*Shabraque of cavaliers, from 1764 to 1796 - Palash, ljadunka and epaulet*      *band of cavaliers, from 1764 to 1796*

*Officer and the seal life guards cavalry regiment, from 1786 to 1796*

*Designed military equipment of the life guards of the cavalry regiment, 1788*

*Cavalry guard, from 1764 to 1796*

*Guard cavalry Officer, from 1764 to 1796*

*Guard cavalry from 1764 to 1796*

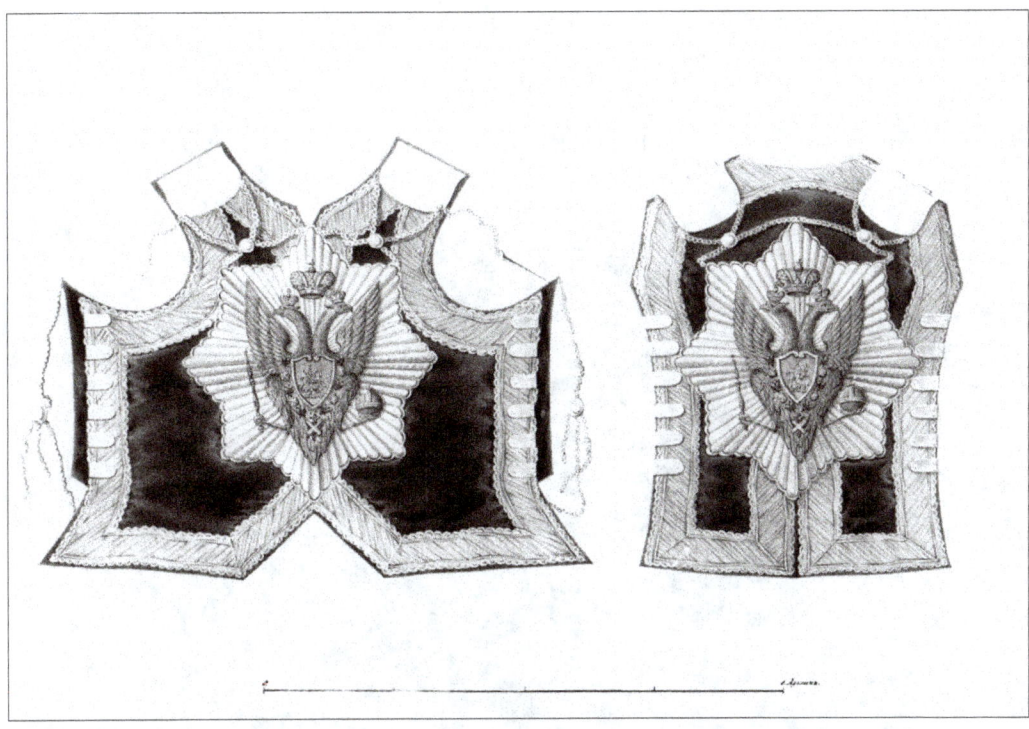

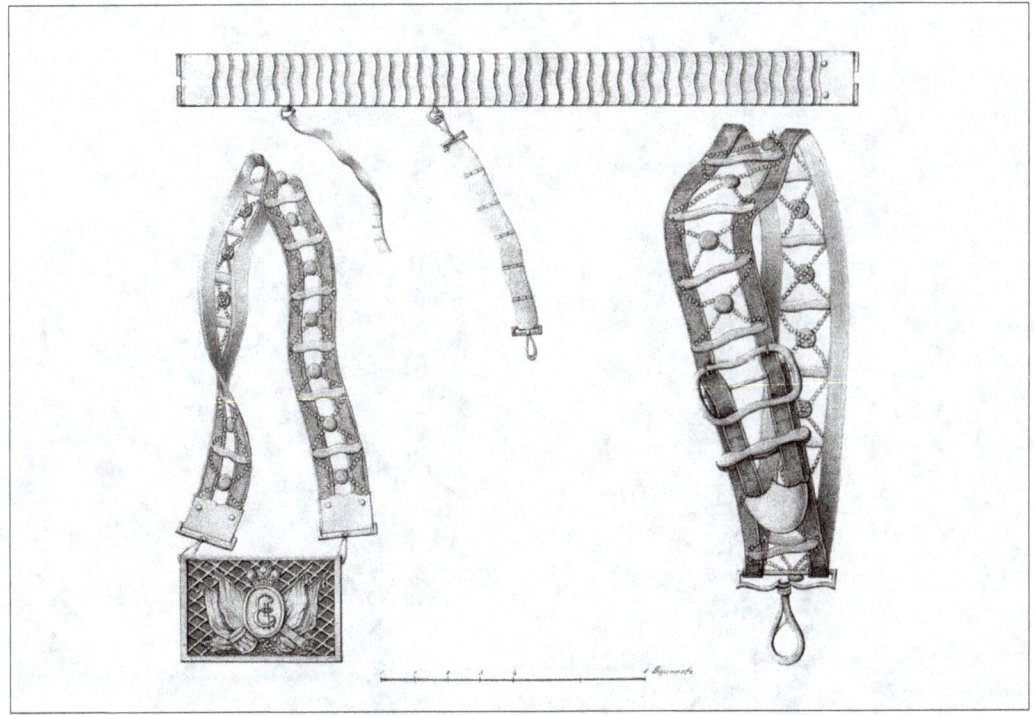

*Parade shabraque of the cavaliers, from 1764 to 1796. Ceremonial: portupeya, ljadunka and   shoulder belt of the cavalry guards from 1764 to 1796*

*Private and Trumpet of the leib-hussar squadron, from 1776 to 1796*

*Private of the leib-hussar squadron, from 1/76 to 1/96*

*Officer and a Private Chuguevskaya cossack convoy command, from 1776 to 1790*

*Radovoy Chuguevskaya convoy cossack team, from 1776 to 1790*

*NCO and the Private Don cossack convoy, from 1776 to 1790*

*Officer of the Don cossack convoy, from 1776 to 1790*

*Officer of Don cossack command, from 1776 to 1790*

*Private and Officer of the Convoy cossack teams, 1790-1796*

*Cadet of the 1ᵗ Age of the Land Cadet Corps, 1767-1796*

*Cadets of the 3ʳᵈ and 2ⁿᵈ ages of the Land Cadet Corps, 1767-1796*

*Cadets of the Land Cadet Corps, from 1767 to 1786*

*Cadets of the Land Cadet Corps, from 1767 to 1786*

*Officers of the Land Cadet Corps, 1767-1786*

*Cadet of the 4ᵗʰ and 5ᵗʰ ages of the Land Cadet Corps, from 1767-1786*

*Cadets of the 3rd age of the Land Cadet Corps*

*Officer and 5ᵗʰ-year Cadet of the Land Cadet Corps, from 1786-1796*

*Baraban of the Land Cadet Corps, 1786-1796*

Cadets of the Artillery and Engineering Cadet Corps, 1762-1784

*Cadets of the Artillery and Engineering Cadet Corps, 1762-1784*

*Bombardir Jaws Cadet of the Artillery, 1762-1796*

*Engineering Cadet Corps, 1762-1796*

*Officers of the Artillery and Engineering Cadet Corps, 1762-1784*

*Cadet of the Artillery and Engineering Cadet Corps, 1784-1796*

*Pupil of the School of Art at the Artillery and Engineering Cadet Corps, 1762-1784*

*Pupil of the School of Art at the Artillery and Engineering Cadet Corps, 1762-1784*

Cadet and Officer of the Artillery and Engineering Cadet Corps, 1784-1786

*Cadet and Officer of the Artillery and Engineering Cadet Corps, 1784-1786*

*Cadets of the Artillery and Engineering Cadet Corps, 1784-1796*

*Officer and Cadet of the Artillery and Engineering Cadet Corps, 1786-1796*

*Ukrainian hussar regiment, from 1776 to 1783*

*Officer of the Gymnasium of the Migrant Mutantners, 1775-1786*

*Vospitannik and Officer of the Gymnasium of the Stranger Mutual believers, 1786-1792*

*Vospitannik Corps of the Migrant Migrant, 1792-1796*

*Officer of the Corps of the Migrant Migrants, 1792-1796*

*Vospitannik Corps of the Stranger Migrant, 1793-1796*

*Veterans of Garrison Battalion, from 1764 to 1786*

*Masterovo Garrison Battalion, from 1764 to 1786*

*Picture of the Garrison Battalion, 1764-1786*

*Garrison General officers, 1764-1780*

*Garrison General Mayor and Garrison Brigadier, 1764-1780*

# SOLDIERS, WEAPONS & UNIFORMS ALREADY PUBLISHED
## (SOME TITLES)

**UNIFORMS OF RUSSIAN ARMY IN THE ERA OF ANCIENT TZAR**
FROM THE REIGN OF VASILI IV TO MICHAEL I, ALEXIS, FEODOR III DURING THE XVII th CENTURY
A.V.VISKOVATOV — LUCA STEFANO CRISTINI
SWU-600-004

**UNIFORMS OF RUSSIAN ARMY OF PETER I THE GREAT**
FROM THE REIGN OF PETER I TO CATHERINE I, PEER II, ANNA AND IVAN VI, 1682-1741
A.V.VISKOVATOV — LUCA STEFANO CRISTINI
SWU-700-006

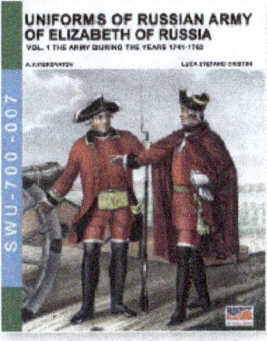

**UNIFORMS OF RUSSIAN ARMY OF ELIZABETH OF RUSSIA**
VOL. 1 THE ARMY DURING THE YEARS 1741-1762
A.V.VISKOVATOV — LUCA STEFANO CRISTINI
SWU-700-007

**UNIFORMS OF RUSSIAN ARMY OF ELIZABETH OF RUSSIA**
VOL. 2 THE ARMY DURING THE YEARS 1741-1762
A.V.VISKOVATOV — LUCA STEFANO CRISTINI
SWU-700-008

**UNIFORMS OF RUSSIAN ARMY IN THE XVIII CENTURY  VOL. 1**
UNDER THE REIGN OF CATHERINE II EMPRESS OF RUSSIA BETWEEN 1762 AND 1796
A.V.VISKOVATOV — LUCA STEFANO CRISTINI
SWU-700-005

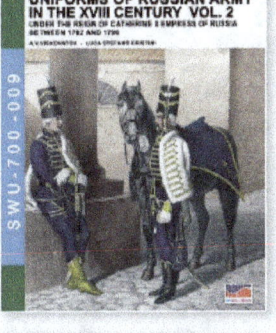

**UNIFORMS OF RUSSIAN ARMY IN THE XVIII CENTURY  VOL. 2**
UNDER THE REIGN OF CATHERINE II EMPRESS OF RUSSIA BETWEEN 1762 AND 1796
A.V.VISKOVATOV — LUCA STEFANO CRISTINI
SWU-700-009

**UNIFORMS OF RUSSIAN ARMY IN THE XVIII CENTURY  VOL. 3**
UNDER THE REIGN OF CATHERINE II EMPRESS OF RUSSIA BETWEEN 1762 AND 1796
A.V.VISKOVATOV — LUCA STEFANO CRISTINI
SWU-700-010

**UNIFORMS OF RUSSIAN ARMY IN THE XVIII CENTURY  VOL. 4**
UNDER THE REIGN OF CATHERINE II EMPRESS OF RUSSIA BETWEEN 1762 AND 1796
A.V.VISKOVATOV — LUCA STEFANO CRISTINI
SWU-700-011

**BRITISH ARMY UNIFORMS IN 1742**
IN THE ART OF JOHN PINE
SWU-700-001

**PRUSSIAN & AUSTRIAN ARMY UNIFORMS IN 1742-1770**
LUCA STEFANO CRISTINI
SWU-700-002

**THE FRENCH ARMY OF ANCIEN RÉGIME Volume 1**
IN THE ART OF FELIX PHILIPPOTEAUX
LUCA STEFANO CRISTINI
SWU-700-003

**THE FRENCH ARMY OF ANCIEN RÉGIME Volume 2**
IN THE ART OF FELIX PHILIPPOTEAUX
LUCA STEFANO CRISTINI
SWU-700-004

**THE EXERCISE OF ARMES**
JACOB DE GHEYN II · LUCA S. CRISTINI
SWU-600-001

**DUTCH & IMPERIAL SOLDIERS**
ADAM VAN BREEN & HENDRICK GOLTZIUS · LUCA S. CRISTINI
SWU-600-002

**HORSEMEN IN THE 16TH & 17TH C.**
JACOB DE GHEYN II · A.DE BRUYN · LUCA S. CRISTINI
SWU-600-003

**IMPERIAL SOLDIERS & UNIFORMS 1640-1860**
IN THE ART OF FRANZ GERASCH
LUCA S.CRISTINI                    Plates by FRANZ GERASCH
SWU-GEN-001